To
Serena:
Remember He is
the Gift

Merry Christmas!

Don & Pearl Anderson

II Cor 9: 15

A Gift too Wonderful for Words

A Gift too Wonderful for Words

Don Anderson

LOIZEAUX BROTHERS

Neptune, New Jersey

First Edition, September 1987

Printed in the United States of America.

A publication of Loizeaux Brothers, Inc.
A nonprofit organization devoted to the Lord's work and to the spread of His truth.

All New Testament Scripture quotations, unless otherwise noted, are taken from the author's personal translation of the Greek text.
References noted NIV are from the *Holy Bible, New International Version,* copyright 1973, 1978, 1984, by the International Bible Society and are used by permission.
References noted NASB are from the *New American Standard Bible,* copyright The Lockman Foundation 1960, 1962, 1963, 1968, 1971, 1972, 1973, 1975, 1977, and are used by permission.
References noted TLB are from *The Living Bible,* copyright 1971 by Tyndale House Publishers, Wheaton, Illinois, and are used by permission.
References noted KJV are from the *Authorized King James Version.*
"The Christmas Tree" by M. B. Bill Dunn is used by permission of the author and publisher, BDC Service Corporation, P.O. Box 922, Euless, TX 76039.

Library of Congress Cataloging-in-Publication Data

Anderson, Don, 1933-
    A gift too wonderful for words.

    Bibliography: p.
    1. Jesus Christ—Nativity.   2. Incarnation.
I. Title.
BT315 2.A525   1987   232.9'2   87-16960
ISBN 0-87213-003-7

The author wishes to acknowledge the editorial assistance of Jane Rodgers.

DEDICATION

To the six gifts God has given me:
Pearl, Donna, Becky, Bobby, Andy, and Julea.

אֲנִי לְדוֹדִי וְדוֹדִי לִי

I am my beloved's, and my beloved is mine
Song of Solomon 6:3

πάντα χαὶ ἐυ πᾶσιυ Χϕιστός

Christ is all and in all
Colossians 3:11

C O N T E N T S

FOREWORD

The Christmas story is much more than a seasonal motif to garnish the Sunday before the Big Day. The entire Old Testament points to the incarnation; the New Testament stems from it. All human history pivots on the miracle of Christ's birth. Of all the marvels recorded in the Bible, including the resurrection, nothing is so majestic to me as the miracle of God Almighty coming to earth in the form of a tiny baby.

In shopping malls Christmas decorations appear before Thanksgiving; entire stores are devoted to selling yuletide items. With countless hours and dollars spent preparing to celebrate, why do we normally eke out only a few minutes from the week before Christmas to read the story from the Bible? Why don't we take a deep look at the reason for our celebration?

A Gift Too Wonderful for Words does exactly that. Bible teacher Don Anderson points the reader to the beginning of the real story in Genesis. He shows how the torch of expectation was relayed from one generation to the next until the coming of the promised Messiah. In an understandable way, he explains why history two thousand years old is vital today.

Don has a unique gift of writing Bible exposition accurately in a style which is enjoyable to read and helpful to teach. This book fits the Sunday School, Bible study, family devotions, and personal worship. I am encouraged to see this long-overdue theme in print. Don and I enjoy a friendship rooted in his student days at seminary and our board relationship directing Pine Cove Conference Center. I hold him and his wife, Pearl, in high esteem.

The author writes of hope. That Christ came just as He

promised raises our highest anticipation for His return—just as He promised. Like an expectant child on Christmas morning, Christians look for Christ's certain second advent. It is this hope which makes *A Gift Too Wonderful for Words* a significant volume as well as a Christmas blessing. When the world's eyes turn to Him in curiosity and wonder, believers may adore Him, worship Him, and trust Him.

HOWARD G. HENDRICKS
Chairman, Center for Christian Leadership
Dallas Theological Seminary

P R E F A C E

"I have much to write to you, but I do not want to use paper and ink. Instead, I hope to visit you and talk with you face to face, so that our joy may be complete" (2 John 12 NIV).

It is everyone's desire at Christmas to be close and to communicate face to face. I wish I could invite you into our home and we could sit by the fire, sipping hot chocolate and sharing the joys of the holidays.

I want to wish you a blessed season, and my prayer is that *A Gift Too Wonderful for Words* will help make this Christmas the best ever. My hope is that this book might assist you in celebrating the season to the glory of God. The last portion of the final chapter is designed for group reading on Christmas morning.

A special thanks is in order to Jane Rodgers for her tireless labors in putting this all together. Jane means "gracious gift of God," and to our Ministries' family, she has been just that. Jan Terry and Jean Powell man the office on the home front and make it all happen, too! Peter Bartlett and Claudia Mooij from Loizeaux Brothers have brought us such joy as well—for their friendship, vision, and commitment to God's Word.

Merry Christmas!

Tracing the Seed

*T*ake a couple of aspirin, slow down, and come see me after the holidays," says the doctor to many of his exhausted patients phoning in their late-December ailments. Why? It's because each Christmas season brings with it its own share of headaches—for everybody.

Simply consider the hassles of shopping. Through ice, wind, rain, and gloom of night, determined drivers hop into metallic steeds to do battle with the horsepower of the streets and parking lots. Duels of the desperate are waged over left-turns, rights-of-way, and parking spaces. With reasonable luck, one's six cylinder beast grinds to a halt in a spot eight hundred yards from the entrance to the mall. Then comes the hike to the glass and chrome gates of retail heaven, where the real fun begins.

Inside the mall, harried Christmas shoppers speed past Salvation Army bell ringers and scurry from store to store, joining a throng of people rushing along crowded corridors, like so many ants swarming within a many-chambered mound. Briskly stepping in time to the Muzak of "Jingle Bells," they pass by hundreds of counters, racks, and fixtures, pausing by more than a few, searching for just the right present. Gold earrings for Mom . . . a velour robe for Dad . . . a tie for Uncle Pete . . . watches and bracelets, VCRs and stereos, toy soldiers and Cabbage Patch dolls.

Lines form in front of cash registers, as weary customers make purchases from overworked clerks. There is a pervasive sense of chaos, and not a great deal of "peace on earth, good will to men," decking the malls at Christmas time. At yuletide even my wife, who was born with a shopping bag in her hand, comes home a *totalled* woman, sick and tired of the traffic congestion outside and inside shopping centers. As the strains of "Silent Night" play in the background, she is desperately wishing for one!

In fact, I'd say that the *peace* of Christmas has largely been replaced by the *press and push* of Christmas in our society. We Americans overdo and overindulge. I'm not just referring to the hustle and bustle of seasonal shopping, either, although by mid-December, most of us are overextended on our charge accounts. I've found that out the hard way, incidentally. Last Christmas, when I tried to charge a last-minute gift, a would-be comedian disguised as a store clerk inquired, "Do you have another credit card? Santa has already danced on that one to your limit!"

Come December, we're not only financially overcommitted, we also find ourselves socially committed to a flurry of holiday parties, and just about ready to be *committed*—plain and simple—to a local hospital for some badly needed R & R! Adding extra church services and activities to the pot makes for a season of busyness, the likes of which our grandparents never imagined.

THE PERFECT, PROMISED GIFT

In the midst of our Christmas card sending and the holiday vending, we may too easily forget that all the hoopla began as the celebration of the birthday of a king, Jesus Christ. God's ultimate gift to us, He is the original, and only truly meaningful, "reason for the season." Thoughts of Him should be on our minds as we give stationary to Grandma and golf balls to Gramps, a nightgown to Aunt Katherine and a hand mixer to cousin Phyllis.

And though many of our earthly presents will wind up at the return counters of department stores on December 26, we need also remember that the gift of Christ is never the wrong size, wrong color, wrong model, or wrong style. Instead, He is God's perfect gift to us. He fits everybody—and He'll never wear out!

Not only that, but the gift of Christ was well planned, and clearly predicted. The coming of the precious Savior whose birth we celebrate should not have been a surprise to any worshiper of God. News of His expected arrival had plainly been revealed in God's Word centuries before the first Christmas Day. He was promised long before He lay as a babe in a manger in Bethlehem.

We're going to look within the sacred page, to see just where some of the prophecies concerning Christ appear. These predictions and others, so tangibly fulfilled in the birth, life, death, and resurrection of Jesus, offer irrefutable evidence that the Bible is much more than a human record of historical events. It is the authoritative Word of God—written over a period of 1600 years, penned by forty-four human authors inspired by the Holy Spirit, telling one story from Genesis to Revelation: the story of God's plan for humanity through the working of Jesus Christ.

As we turn to some of the major prophetic passages concerning Christ in Scripture, my hope and prayer is that the brief overview contained in this chapter will enrich your celebration this Christmas season, and in the years to come. Let's look now at what God's Word has to say.

THE NEED AND THE SEED

Our story opens in an unspeakably lush and beautiful setting—the garden of Eden, where all serenity has just been shattered by the ugliness of human sin. Adam and Eve have violated the single commandment given them by their Creator: they have eaten forbidden fruit from the tree in the very middle of their paradise. In Genesis 3:15 we read of God's judgment upon the serpent who has tempted and deceived the woman in the garden. "And I will put enmity between you and the woman, and between your offspring and hers; he will crush your head, and you will strike his heel" (NIV), says the Lord God to Satan, the person possessing the power behind the serpent. The sin committed by Adam and Eve in the midst of Eden's perfection demands justice. Yet a righteous and holy God, who could easily have washed His hands of all further dealings with the disobedient humans He has created, chooses instead to include a marvelous promise and provision in His pronouncement of judgment.

That promise involves a seed. God warns the serpent, or Satan, that this coming seed will crush the evil one's head, though Satan will "strike his heel" (3:15). In other words, this promised seed, this special person, will engage in a struggle of eternal proportions with the devil, and will emerge victorious. Thus there is hope for the fallen human race, after all! But how does God plan to bring this Holy One into the world?

The beginnings of the answer to that question can be found in Genesis 12. Centuries after the gates of Eden are slammed shut to sinful men and women, the Lord calls forth for Himself a people, a chosen race: the Jews. The first of these is an obscure sheepmaster from an insignificant town: Abram from Ur of the Chaldees. As Genesis 12:1-3 reveals, God commands Abram to leave Ur, saying:

> Go forth from your country,
> And from your relatives

And from your father's house,
To the land which I will show you;
And I will make you a great nation,
And I will bless you,
And make your name great;
And so you shall be a blessing;
And I will bless those who bless you,
And the one who curses you I will curse.
And in you all the families of the earth shall be
    blessed (NASB).

Essentially, God tells Abram to depart from his home town and journey to a land he does not know. Once there, the Lord intends to enter into a covenant relationship with the man. The provisions of this relationship, which we know as the Abrahamic Covenant, involve a seed and a land, and include the promises that Abram is going to become "a great nation," and that through him "all the families of the earth" are going to be "blessed." It is to be through the family line of Abram that the seed promised in Genesis 3:15 will come. Some of us hope that our children or grandchildren will become presidents. Abram—whom we will refer to as Abraham, "the father of many nations," the name he will soon be known by—looks forward to something far greater for one of his descendants.

There is a catch to this promise, though. At the time when God speaks to him in Ur, Abraham has no children. Not only that, but the prospects of his ever having any sons or daughters seem pretty dim. He is seventy-five, his wife only ten years younger . . . and they've long given up on the idea of starting a family. Coping with infertility has become a way of life for them.

The baby boom in Abraham's household doesn't happen immediately, either. In fact, God doesn't intend for it to take place for a quarter of a century. Ten years pass . . . Abraham's wife, Sarah, sees she isn't getting any younger, so she convinces her husband to follow the custom of the day, and use one of her handmaids, a woman named Hagar, as a kind of surrogate mother. The union of Abraham and Hagar produces a son, Ishmael, but he is not the child God has in mind. Fifteen more barren years slip by for Sarah, and finally, in Genesis 17:19, the Lord speaks to Abraham, saying: "Yes, but your wife Sarah will bear you a son, and you will call him Isaac. I will establish my covenant with him as an everlasting covenant for his descendants after him" (NIV). And within a year, the bouncing baby Isaac is born to his doting, delighted, but elderly, parents.

Although Abraham remarries after Sarah's death, and fathers other children besides Isaac and Ishmael (see Genesis 25), it is through Isaac that the line of promise continues. Using much the same words He had earlier spoken to Abraham, the Lord eventually appears to Isaac and confirms His intentions with this statement:

> For to you and your descendants I will give all these lands and will confirm the oath I swore to your father Abraham. I will make your descendants as numerous as the stars in the sky and will give them all these lands, and through your offspring all nations on earth will be blessed (Genesis 26:3-4 NIV).

God's covenant with Isaac, as with Abraham, is unconditional. Its fulfillment depends upon God alone, not on anything man might do. The descendants of Abraham will not receive God's blessings because of their exemplary behavior or adherence to a list of rules and regulations. They will be able to do nothing to earn their standing as God's chosen people! As always the fulfillment of the Lord's promises depends upon Him, and Him alone! After all, it is His reputation and character which are at stake.

In the course of time, Isaac and his wife Rebekah become the parents of twin boys, Esau and Jacob. It is the younger son, Jacob, who is selected by God, and through whom the line of the promised seed can be traced.

Jacob's marital history could provide enough risque material to fill the scripts of a dozen soap operas. Between his two wives and two concubines, he fathers a whole tentful of children. His twelve sons become the patriarchs of what is known as the twelve tribes of the nation of Israel. Of the twelve, it will be through the family of Jacob's fourth-born son, Judah, that the line of the promised seed will continue.

Genesis 49:10 records that, as Jacob lies on his deathbed and his sons are gathered around him to hear his final words, he announces this: "The scepter shall not depart from Judah, Nor the ruler's staff from between his feet, Until Shiloh comes" (NASB). The word *Shiloh,* meaning "rest" or "tranquility," signifies the Messiah, the promised seed, and indicates a time when God's presence will be among men. The scepter and ruler's staff symbolize royalty, the trappings of a king. And as predicted by his father Jacob, Judah's descendants become the tribe of kings, the ultimate issue of which is Shiloh, the King of kings, the seed first promised in Genesis 3:15.

The Tribe of Kings

We learn more about the coming King in Numbers 24:17, where Balaam reveals what the Lord has made known to him, "A star will come out of Jacob: a scepter will rise out of Israel" (NIV). This scepter, this star, which is to come from the family of Jacob and his son Judah, will be royalty indeed. He will be called the Lion of the tribe of Judah. Yet before His arrival, other kings and princes will be found among Judah's descendants.

Perhaps the greatest of these is David, a shepherd anointed by God to become the second king of Israel, the successor to Saul. As He enters into a covenant relationship with Abraham, so God also establishes a covenant with David, which we refer to as the Davidic Covenant. Not only will the line of the seed promised in Genesis 3:15 continue through David, but one of his descendants will sit on the throne of a kingdom which will endure forever and ever.

Under David's military genius, the nation of Israel expands enormously. Following the Israelite defeat of the Philistines, David orders that the ark containing the very Spirit of the Lord be brought from its obscure resting place into the city of Jerusalem, the recently-proclaimed capitol and religious center of the land (see 2 Samuel 6). David—a man who deeply desires to honor God—soon senses the irony of the fact that he lives in a plush palace of cedar, while the ark of the Lord remains housed in a tent within the city walls. The king, determined to order the construction of a grand temple to house the ark, reveals his intentions to the prophet Nathan, who at first wholeheartedly agrees (see 2 Samuel 7:1-3).

But as it so often happens, God has other ideas. The Lord reveals His wishes to Nathan on the same night in which David has expressed his hopes for building the temple. First of all, God tells Nathan that He has never asked David or any other Israelite leader to erect an earthly house for Him (see 2 Samuel 7:5-7). Then the Lord goes on to say to the prophet:

> Now then, tell my servant David, "This is what the LORD Almighty says: I took you from the pasture and from following the flock to be ruler over my people Israel. I have been with you wherever you have gone, and I have cut off all your enemies from before you. Now I will make your name great, like the names of the greatest men of the earth. And I will provide a place for my people Israel and will plant them so that they can have a home of their own and no longer be disturbed. Wicked people will not oppress them anymore, as they did at the beginning and have done ever since the time I appointed leaders over my people Israel. I will also give you rest from all your enemies (2 Samuel 7:8-11 NIV).

After telling Nathan to remind David of all that He had done for him, God makes some splendid promises. First of all, David's name will be great (7:9), which it surely is, even to this day. Moreover, the Lord pledges that He will provide a place—a specific land—for the children of Israel, where they will be able to live in peace (7:10). Thus David will know that his efforts to subdue resistance in the promised land will meet with success, and that the Israelites will enjoy rest in the land of their fathers. Then God continues to speak to Nathan, instructing him to inform David that:

> The LORD declares to you that the LORD himself will establish a house for you: When your days are over and you rest with your fathers, I will raise up your offspring to succeed you, who will come from your own body, and I will establish his kingdom. He is the one who will build a house for my Name, and I will establish the throne of his kingdom forever. I will be his father, and he will be my son. When he does wrong, I will punish him with the rod of men, with floggings inflicted by men. But my love will never be taken away from him, as I took it away from Saul, whom I removed from before you. Your house and your kingdom will endure forever before me; your throne will be established forever (2 Samuel 7:12-16 NIV).

The Lord intends to establish a "house"—a royal kingdom and dynasty—for David. David's name will be great, yes, but far greater will be the name of one of his descendants in this royal dynasty. Who will this man be? Some think that the prophetic promise refers to Solomon, David's son and successor. Indeed, Solomon later builds an elaborate temple to contain the ark of the Lord (see 2 Chronicles 3–4). Yet it is not recorded in Scripture that Solomon ever experiences physical punishment "with the rod of men, with floggings inflicted by men." And the rule of a mortal man such as

Solomon could never be "established forever," could it?

No, the descendant promised to David in 2 Samuel 7:12-16 is not his son Solomon, but a "greater son." This greater son, Jesus Christ, would walk upon the earth centuries after the time of David. He would be known to the world as the oldest offspring of the carpenter Joseph, a descendant of David (see Matthew 1:1-16). He would be known to those who called Him Lord as the virgin-born Son of God. It would be Christ who would suffer at the hands of men, and one day it will be the same Christ who will return again to earth, and whose eternal kingdom God the Father will establish. As the apostle John foretells in Revelation 11:15, the day will come when voices from heaven will arise to proclaim: "The kingdom of the world has become the kingdom of our Lord, and of His Christ; and He will reign forever and ever" (NASB).

When Nathan reports God's marvelous words to David, the king's reaction is one of praise and thanksgiving. "For this reason Thou art great, O LORD GOD; for there is none like Thee, and there is no God besides Thee, according to all that we have heard with our ears," exclaims the king in 2 Samuel 7:22 (NASB). Does David realize that the ultimate fulfillment of all that the Lord has promised will be in the person of the God-man, Jesus Christ? Surely he does not grasp all of the implications of God's covenant with him. And yet centuries later, Jesus Christ comes down to dwell among men. By His death, He offers life to all who will believe on Him (see John 3:16, Romans 5:8-12). And thus He strikes a fatal blow to Satan's grip upon the human race. The initial coming of this King of kings, the seed first promised in the garden of Eden, is what we rightfully celebrate on Christmas Day.

PROMISES, PROMISES

Let's learn more about this Christ, this promised seed, by looking at some of the over three hundred biblical prophecies concerning His birth, life, death, resurrection, and second coming. Each prophetic utterance is something like a dot found on one of the connect-the-dot pictures we did as kids. Follow the "dots" of scriptural prophecy, and you'll wind up with a beautiful portrait of the Savior. We'll be briefly touching on merely a few of these predictions; some will be covered in more detail in the next chapter.

As we continue to turn the pages of Scripture, considering some of its books in order, I hope it will become obvious to you that Christ is the thread binding together the books of the Old and New Testaments. He literally is a stream of life running through all, unifying, cementing together the magnificent volume we know as the Bible.

BORN TO DIE

Psalms 16 and 22 are among the many songs written by King David, who, besides being a military mastermind, was also a gifted writer, poet, lyricist, and musician. Portions of these two psalms are prophetic in nature, as we shall see.

In Psalm 16:10, we read, "For Thou wilt not abandon my soul to Sheol: Neither wilt Thou allow Thy Holy One to undergo decay" (NASB). Just as God would not eternally sentence David's soul to Sheol, the place of the dead, neither would He condemn the coming Holy One of the Lord to endure decay. The prophetic language is a prediction of the resurrection of this Holy One, this promised seed, this Christ who was born to die for us . . . and who would not suffer everlasting death (see Acts 2:21, 13:35). He it is who has risen from the dead, and who eventually will rule eternally, fulfilling the "forevers" in the promise of God to David in 2 Samuel 7.

Turning a few pages in our Bibles, we find the drama of Psalm 22. With agonized voice, David laments of his own sufferings in verse 1, "My God, my God, why hast Thou forsaken me? Far from my deliverance are the words of my groaning" (NASB). His words transport us to the foot of Calvary, where Jesus Christ, hanging upon the cross, also loudly cries in anguish, "Eli, Eli, lama sabachthani?" or "My God, My God, why hast Thou forsaken Me?" (Matthew 27:46 NASB). The prophetic parallel is unmistakable . . . David's words foreshadow the heart-and-soul-wrenching message of our Savior.

And yet that is not all, for further along in Psalm 22, as David continues to write of his suffering, we are also given a searing and painful picture of the horrors of crucifixion. It is amazing to realize that these words were penned seven hundred years before Christ met His death upon the cross. David and his countrymen did not practice crucifixion as a form of punishment, and were not likely to have been intimately acquainted with the rigors of this method of execution. But through the inspiration of the Holy Spirit, David was able to describe with remarkable and terrifying accuracy the agony experienced by our Lord at Calvary. Beginning with verse 14 of Psalm 22, we read the graphic account:

> I am poured out like water,
> And all my bones are out of joint;
> My heart is like wax;
> It is melted within me.
> My strength is dried up like a potsherd,
> And my tongue cleaves to my jaws;
> And Thou dost lay me in the dust of death.
> For dogs have surrounded me;
> A band of evildoers has encompassed me;
> They pierced my hands and my feet.
> I can count all my bones.
> They look, they stare at me;
> They divide my garments among them,
> And for my clothing they cast lots
> (Psalm 22:14-18 NASB).

While surely David underwent trial and persecution, he was never crucified. Consider briefly how his words mirror what would actually happen to his greatest descendant, Jesus Christ, seven hundred years later.

> *"I am poured out like water, And all my bones are out of joint. . . ."* The trauma of crucifixion included the horrid fact that one's body weight gradually pulled joint from joint, tearing muscle and sinew in unimaginable agony.

> *"My strength is dried up like a potsherd, And my tongue cleaves to my jaws. . . ."* None can doubt that Jesus' strength was drained by the brutal beatings He received at the hands of His captors, the demanding journey to the brow of Golgotha, the hours upon the cross. As the moment of His death approached, Christ requested something to drink. John 19:28 tells us that a sponge soaked in wine vinegar was lifted to His lips. When He received this drink, He proclaimed, "'It is finished' . . . bowed his head and gave up his spirit" (John 19:30 NIV).

> *"A band of evildoers has encompassed me; They pierced my hands and my feet. . . . They look, they stare at me; They divide my garments among them, And for my clothing they cast lots."* The words of Mark 15:24 eloquently testify to the fulfillment of this prophetic utterance, speaking of the Roman soldiers who nailed Christ to the cross: "And they crucified Him, and divided up His garments among themselves, casting lots for them, to decide what each should take" (NASB).

This Jesus, this "greater son" of David, was a man born to die, and in so dying He fulfilled the over three hundred specific Old Testament predictions alluded to earlier. We have seen but a smattering of the prophecies pertaining to the Savior. As we continue to flip through the pages of Scripture, let's look briefly at a few more of the hundreds of passages relevant to the Messiah's mission on earth.

The biblical writings of the men we know as the major and minor prophets were recorded during a time span from approximately seven hundred years before Christ till 400-450 B.C. The work of the prophet Isaiah, for example, is dated anywhere from 740 to 680 B.C., while the writings of Malachi, whose book marks the end of the Old Testament, are believed to have been produced sometime during the years 400 to 450 B.C.

It is amazing to examine the prophetic statements made by such men centuries before the coming of Christ, and then to turn to the pages of the New Testament and read how each Old Testament prediction was undeniably and specifically fulfilled in Christ Jesus. Merely a few of the striking Old Testament prophecies concerning the birth, life, death, and resurrection of Christ, are reprinted below, with Scripture references from the New Testament indicating passages recording the fulfillment of each prophecy. For a far more complete listing, I recommend chapter nine of Josh McDowell's *Evidence That Demands a Verdict* (Campus Crusade for Christ, 1972). For now, my hope is that the brief list beginning below will give you more than just food for thought, but meat for meditation . . . and cause for worship this Christmas Day, and every day.

PROPHECIES FULFILLED IN CHRIST

Here, in the order in which they appear in the Bible, are some of the Old Testament prophecies concerning Christ, with the New Testament references showing their fulfillment.

Jesus' Virgin Birth and Naming

Old Testament Prophecy *New Testament Fulfillment*
Isaiah 7:14 *Matthew 1:18, 23-25*

Therefore the LORD Himself will give you a sign: Behold, a virgin will be with child and bear a son, and she will call His name Immanuel (Isaiah 7:14 NASB).

Jesus' First Advent as a Child, and Second Coming as the Eternal Prince of Peace

Old Testament Prophecy *New Testament Fulfillment*
Isaiah 9:6-7 *Luke 1:32, 2:11;*
Revelation 19–21

For a child will be born to us, a son will be given to us; And the government will rest on His shoulders; And His name will be called Wonderful Counselor, Mighty God, Eternal Father, Prince of Peace. There will be no end to the increase of His government or of peace, On the throne of David and over his kingdom, To establish it and to uphold it with justice and righteousness from then on and forevermore. The zeal of the LORD of hosts will accomplish this.
(Isaiah 9:6-7 NASB)

The Messiah as a Descendant of Jesse, the Father of David

Old Testament Prophecy *New Testament Fulfillment*
Isaiah 11:1 *Luke 3:23-32;*
Matthew 1:6-16

A shoot will come up from the stump of Jesse; from his roots a Branch will bear fruit (Isaiah 11:1 NIV).

29

The Coming of John the Baptist to Prepare the Way for
the Public Ministry of Jesus

Old Testament Prophecy   *New Testament Fulfillment*
Isaiah 40:1-3   *Matthew 3:1-3; Luke 1:17;*
                                    John 1:23

The voice of him that crieth in the wilderness,
Prepare ye the way of the LORD, make straight in
the desert a highway for our God (Isaiah 40:3
KJV).

Christ as a Man of Sorrows, Despised by Men, Rejected by
His Own People

Old Testament Prophecy   *New Testament Fulfillment*
Isaiah 53:3   *John 1:11, 7:5,48*

He is despised and rejected of men; a man of
sorrows, and acquainted with grief: and we hid as
it were our faces from him: he was despised, and
we esteemed him not (Isaiah 53:3 KJV).

Christ Crushed and Scourged

Old Testament Prophecy   *New Testament Fulfillment*
Isaiah 53:5   *Matthew 27:26*

But He was pierced through for our transgressions, He was crushed for our iniquities; The chastening for our well-being fell upon Him, And by
His scourging we are healed (Isaiah 53:5 NASB).

Jesus as the Bearer of Our Sins

Old Testament Prophecy   *New Testament Fulfillment*
Isaiah 53:6   *John 1:29,*
                                    1 Corinthians 15:3

But the LORD has caused the iniquity of us all To
fall on Him (Isaiah 53:6b NASB).

Christ's Silence before His Accusers

Old Testament Prophecy   *New Testament Fulfillment*
Isaiah 53:7   *Matthew 27:12-19*

He was oppressed and He was afflicted, Yet He did not open His mouth (Isaiah 53:7a NASB).

Jesus' Burial in the Tomb of a Wealthy Man

Old Testament Prophecy   *New Testament Fulfillment*
Isaiah 53:9   *Matthew 27:57-60*

His grave was assigned with wicked men, Yet He was with a rich man in His death (Isaiah 53:9a NASB).

Christ as the Righteous Branch of the Family of David

Old Testament Prophecy   *New Testament Fulfillment*
Jeremiah 23:5   *Luke 3:23-31*

Behold, the days come, saith the Lord, that I will raise unto David a righteous Branch, and a King shall reign and prosper, and shall execute judgment and justice in the earth (Jeremiah 23:5 KJV).

Jesus' Birth at Bethlehem

Old Testament Prophecy   *New Testament Fulfillment*
Micah 5:2   *Matthew 2:1*

But as for you, Bethlehem Ephrathah, Too little to be among the clans of Judah, From you One will go forth for Me to be ruler in Israel. His goings forth are from long ago, From the days of eternity (Micah 5:2 NASB).

The First Palm Sunday: Christ's Entrance into Jerusalem while Riding a Donkey

Old Testament Prophecy   *New Testament Fulfillment*
Zechariah 9:9   *Luke 19:35-37*

Rejoice greatly, O daughter of Zion! Shout in triumph, O daughter of Jerusalem! Behold, your king is coming to you; He is just and endowed with salvation, Humble, and mounted on a donkey, Even on a colt, the foal of a donkey (Zechariah 9:9 NASB).

One of Jesus' Missions: Cleansing the Temple

Old Testament Prophecy   *New Testament Fulfillment*
Malachi 3:1-2   *Matthew 21:12*

And the LORD, whom you seek, will suddenly come to His temple; and the messenger of the covenant, in whom you delight, behold, He is coming (Malachi 3:1 NASB)

PUTTING IT ALL TOGETHER

During the Christmas season, our Ministries office receives more requests for sermons and messages focusing on tracing the seed of Jesus Christ through Scripture than any other subject. What seems to me to be a dry recitation of Bible verses stirs the hearts and minds of hundreds of believers each year. They thrill at the sacred thread that holds it all together. There are several reasons why this is true.

First of all, God's Word is alive and powerful, and it communicates like nothing else. The Lord invented communication, after all, and if we are receptive, then His teachings can come alive for us with the timeless truths of which they are made. They are the very voice of God!

Additionally, the tragic reality is that so many people, even Christians, do not realize that God's Word is bound together by the unifying cord of Jesus Christ. News of His coming is found throughout the Old Testament, and it is thrilling to view the specific fulfillment in Christ of centuries-old prophecies. We are comforted, as we realize that our God is dependable, faithful to work as He says He will. In the words of Joshua 21:45, "Not one of all the LORD's good promises to the house of Israel failed; every one was fulfilled" (NIV).

God has certainly worked as He said He would in sending Jesus, "the son of David, the son of Abraham" (Matthew 1:1 KJV) to earth. Born of a virgin, born in a small village, born to die for us, He was rightly called Immanuel, "God with us" (see Matthew 1:25).

It is vital that this Jesus, this Immanuel, this greatest seed of Abraham and David, reigns in our hearts as the reason for the Christmas season. I pray that the rest of the messages in this book will cause you to rejoice in His power and grace and love. The prophets of old merely looked for His coming . . . we have the opportunity to meet Him face to face as we come to Him in faith. Please, read on.

Reflections for the season

1. Jesus is the original, and only truly meaningful, "reason for the season."

2. Christ is the seed promised in Genesis 3:15, the "greater son" promised to David, and the Savior promised to us all.

3. Over three hundred biblical prophecies were specifically fulfilled in the birth, life, death, and resurrection of Jesus, the Messiah.

Christ in the Prophets

*C*hristmas is usually an occasion of great rejoicing and gladness. Friends and relatives gather for times of togetherness, cramming a year's worth of catching-up into the conversations of a week. It's a time for family. Sleep and schedule are forgotten for a few days.

As our own kids began to move out on their own, Pearl and I asked them to set aside each even-numbered year, if possible, to come home for the holidays. How much we look forward to these reunions with our five children, their spouses, and, of course, the all-important grandchildren! Nearly everyone was able to make it home for Christmas of '86, and it was a terrific time. Christmas of '87, I fear, will not contain the same measure of pleasure.

You see, as I begin this chapter, my father lies gravely ill with cancer in a rest home in Oregon, some three thousand miles away from my home in Texas. The ominous label "terminal" has been attached to his condition, and in recent weeks his physicians have taken him off of all medication. He is waiting to die. This is a painful time for my family—and I feel especially helpless, because my mom doesn't want me to come. She is afraid that when my dad sees me, knowing that

I've traveled such a long way, he'll believe that she has lost hope.

So, Dad and I talk on the phone. And I tell him that I love him. And I take comfort in the fact that my sister is with Mom, and that my brother lives in nearby Portland. I thank God for the years I've had with my father, but I also realize that by the time next December rolls around, it is highly likely that graduation day will have come for Dad, and he will be celebrating his first Christmas in his eternal dwelling. He won't be around to concoct the homemade divinity, fudge, peanut brittle, and pies he so loved to make for the holidays. Next year, and for several thereafter, our Christmases will be bittersweet, characterized by a blend of joyous recollection, painful reminiscence, and pervaded by a subtle sense of loss. Christmas is like that sometimes.

When a family experiences the loss of a loved one—parent, husband, wife, child, close relative, or friend—there are adjustments to make. Especially during the few years following a tragedy such as death or divorce, holiday celebrations are tinged with sadness, the happiness dulled by moments of heartache. The sense of loss may even bring on depression and, in some, thoughts of suicide.

I guess this irony particularly hit me a few years ago when three men—good men, good friends, vibrant Christians, active churchmen—passed away within a few weeks of each other, just as the Christmas season was gaining momentum. We were ready to round the corner into the final stretch of activities—church events, shopping, caroling, eating, and wrapping—when Woody, Joe, and Cliff finished their courses upon this earth, and slipped into eternity. Forty-mile-per-hour winds and six-degree temperatures make graveside services on Christmas Eve very difficult. The chill goes deeper than the bone.

Christmas that year was bittersweet. Yet there was a precious sense of joy in knowing that it was not truly the end for these men. Woody, Cliff, and Joe had simply experienced the beginning—the beginning of the portion of their eternal lives which they will spend in the presence of God.

Not only is there comfort in knowing where our loved ones who know Christ as Savior will spend eternity, but it is also comforting to realize that God foreordains our lifespans on earth. All our days are known to Him, and He holds all the circumstances of our lives in His controlling hand. He has already mapped out our journeys, determined our destinations, and confirmed our departure dates and times. As David exclaims to the Lord in Psalm 139:16, "All the days ordained for me were written in your book before one of them came to be" (NIV, see also James 4:14-17).

Because of His unconditional love and by an act of His grace, God, through the coming of His Son Jesus Christ, has provided us with a means of living with Him when eternity dawns. In words of Christ Himself in John 14:6, "I am the way, and the truth, and the life; no one comes to the Father, but through Me" (NASB).

Jesus—The Lifeline Anchored to the House

To more deeply know Christ, we must know His Word. . . and that works both ways, for to truly understand His Word, the Bible, we must clearly understand the importance of Jesus Christ within the Scriptures.

I am reminded of an incident from the great northwest. Winters in the northern United States and Canada are fierce. Howling winds whip torrents of snow, creating blizzards of blinding sub-zero whiteness. In the wilderness during pioneer days, venturing a mere six steps from the door of one's home during a snowstorm sometimes proved to be fatal. It was dangerously easy to lose one's bearings even a few feet from the doorway, while all vision of the house evaporated in the whirling whiteness. On the days after blizzards, many a settler was found dead, frozen in a snowbank, sometimes not more than three yards from his home.

Weather could be life-threatening, and posed a particular dilemma for farmers. Even during deadly snowstorms, cows must be milked and stock fed—no farmer worth his salt would willingly neglect his animals, regardless of the personal risk. So, during the early days, farmers who wished to survive the winter made a practice of running a sturdy rope from cabin to barn. The rope, tied securely to both buildings, functioned as a literal lifeline. When the farmers of the north country would tread into the ripping wind and raging ice and snow, they would grip the rope lifeline, knowing that by holding onto it, they would safely make it to the barn and back.

Christ, for us, is a lot like that lifeline. By clinging to Him we will safely traverse the pitfalls of life and arrive at our final destination, with Him. But in addition to being our personal conductor on our journeys through this world, He is the rope of life running throughout Scripture.

Many people feel that they cannot understand the Bible, that it is a perplexing and disjointed discourse, the illogical ravings of men. It is as obscure to them as a house completely hidden by masses of wind-blown snow. But by viewing Christ as the rope of life binding together the books of Scripture, we find the secret to comprehending the Bible. Jesus is the key to unlocking the mysteries of the biblical text, for God's Word is largely God's message to us about His wonderful Son.

It became obvious to God that He would have to intervene directly in human history, and He did so by sending His Son, God incarnate, to earth. In the Bible, that God-man, Christ, is spoken of from Genesis to Revelation. He is the coming Holy One foreshadowed by the prophets. He is pictured in the tabernacle of Exodus, the typology of the book of Leviticus, and the sacrificial system of the Old Testament. He is the voice of the psalms. He is the seed promised in Genesis 3, the Son dying on Golgotha in Matthew 27, and the Savior reigning in glory in Revelation 19. He is King of kings and Lord of lords. As the apostle Paul puts it in Colossians 3:11, "Christ is all, and in all" (NASB).

As we prepare to celebrate the birth of God's greatest gift to us this Christmas season, it is my privilege to introduce you to four men: Isaiah, Jeremiah, Micah, and Zechariah. These four, whose prophecies we considered briefly in chapter one, lived hundreds of years before Jesus came to earth as God incarnate. Their writings are collected in books of the Bible bearing their names. Inspired by the Holy Spirit, they penned the words that we shall examine in this chapter. Their messages were designed to prepare God's people for the coming of His Son. Now these same writings can serve to prepare us to celebrate the birthday of the Lord Jesus Christ, God become flesh.

Isaiah—Of Signs Past and Signs to Come

The prophet Isaiah lived in Jerusalem over seven hundred years before the birth of Christ. His writings spanned the reigns of four kings, and are considered the most beautiful and brilliant produced by the Old Testament prophets. As his words eloquently show, Isaiah battled the religious, moral, political, and social decay plaguing Judah. Vainly he strove to turn the nation toward God, and then boldly predicted her downfall and the preservation of a godly remnant of her people (see Isaiah 6:13). Yet Isaiah's prophecies are far from simply messages of doom and gloom, for rays of hope concerning the first and second comings of the Savior, the Messiah, shimmer throughout.

Hebrews 11:37 speaks of God-fearing men and women who were killed for their faith, "stoned . . . sawed in two . . . tempted . . . put to death with the sword," and so forth. Tradition has it that Isaiah eventually suffered such a martyr's death, being sawed in half. If so, how ironic it is that he would predict the coming of the One who was to become a sacrifice, a martyr for us all, Jesus Christ! In fact, Isaiah refers so many times to the first and second advents of Christ the Messiah, that he is known as the messianic prophet. Let's take an in-depth look at some of his predictions.

SIGNS PAST—ISAIAH 7:14

The first of the passages we're going to consider is found in Isaiah 7:14, where the prophet writes:

> Therefore the Lord himself will give you a sign: The virgin will be with child and will give birth to a son, and will call him Immanuel (NIV).

Notice that the first thing Isaiah predicts is that God will give His children a "sign." When we think of a sign, we think of a traffic sign giving us instructions: telling us to stop, to yield the right of way, to exit left for Highway 45. Or we think of a sign advertising a store, a restaurant, a newscast, a sporting event, or a political candidate. In short, we think of a sign as a large label or as a direction-giver. Neither of these, however, is the sort of sign meant by Isaiah.

In the Bible, the word *sign* refers to a token, an indication, a distinguishing mark of something. Usually a biblical sign consists of a dramatic, miraculous, sovereign intervention into the normal pattern of affairs (i.e., see Matthew 12:38-40). The sign is something tangible to make us realize that God means business, and that He is at work in what is taking place. The miraculous sign recorded in Isaiah 7:14 consists of three parts. Let's consider these.

PART ONE: THE VIRGIN

First of all, Isaiah writes: "The virgin will be with child" (NIV). Notice that the text says, "*The* virgin." No other virgins will ever be with child; there is only one. And when this virgin is pregnant, that will be a sign from God, because virgins don't naturally have babies. According to the normal pattern of things, men and women come together and children are born. This has been true throughout history, except for one occasion and one occasion only: the occasion revealed to Isaiah by the Lord.

The virgin birth spoken of in Isaiah 7:14 did not happen during the prophet's lifetime. It took place some 750 years later, in a stable in a small village. It involved the supernatural intervention into human affairs by a loving and all-powerful God. It was, in other words, a miracle.

The idea that a virgin birth could have taken place is the subject of doubt and scorn by many. Skeptical scholars attempt to discount the virgin birth; many liberal preachers deny that it ever occurred. The launching pads for their expressions of doubt are the very pulpits of America. But how interesting it is that a man of science, a physician, a man knowledgeable in obstetrics and gynecology and thoroughly trained in the workings of the human body, expressed no doubts about the reality of the virgin birth when he wrote of it in one of the Gospels!

Luke is the man of medicine to whom I refer. Dr. Luke had no cynical questions or intellectual reservations about whether it was possible that Christ was born of a virgin. The good doctor was completely convinced that the supernatural birth had occurred. He writes the following in chapter 1 of his Gospel:

> In the sixth month, God sent the angel Gabriel to Nazareth, a town in Galilee, to a virgin pledged to be married to a man named Joseph, a descendant of David. The virgin's name was Mary. The angel went to her and said, "Greetings, you who are highly favored! The Lord is with you."
>
> Mary was greatly troubled at his words and won-

dered what kind of greeting this might be. But the angel said to her, "Do not be afraid, Mary, you have found favor with God. You will be with child and give birth to a son, and you are to give him the name Jesus" (Luke 1:26-31 NIV).

Luke reveals that Mary was surprised at the news of her coming pregnancy. In amazement, she asked of the angel, "How will this be . . . since I am a virgin?" (Luke 1:34 NIV). And the angel replied:

The Holy Spirit will come upon you, and the power of the Most High will overshadow you. So the holy one to be born will be called the Son of God. . . . For nothing is impossible with God" (Luke 1:35-37 NIV).

The angel's last statement explains it all: nothing is impossible with God! We don't have to justify the virgin birth. We don't have to argue and defend it. We just have to accept it, and realize that God told Isaiah that it was going to happen 750 years before it actually did. Galatians 4:4 says, "But when the fulness of the time was come, God sent forth his Son, made of a woman, made under the law" (KJV). And that "fulness of time," that moment of our precious Savior's birth, is the supernatural sign which we choose to commemorate each December 25.

Part Two—The Son

God is often very specific in His revelations. Not only did He tell Isaiah that a virgin would one day give birth to a child, but, as Isaiah continues to relate in verse 14, He also revealed that the baby would be a male. That is part two of his prophecy. Centuries before the virgin's womb became full,

Isaiah knew that a baby boy would be born.

We find record of the fulfillment of this prophecy in Luke 2:6-7, where we read that Mary "gave birth to her first-born son; and she wrapped Him in cloths, and laid Him in a manger, because there was no room for them in the inn" (NASB). Were she from another culture, perhaps Mary would have spent some time knitting blue booties and sweaters in her prenatal months, because long before sonagrams or amniocentesis tests were developed to determine the sex of unborn babies, she knew without doubt that she would bear a son. The angel Gabriel had told her, and Isaiah had prophesied it in the writings of old.

PART THREE—THE NAME

The third part of Isaiah's prophecy concerning the birth of Christ concerns the name which was to be given the babe. Isaiah writes of the virgin and her son: "She will call His name Immanuel" (7:14 NASB). We read in Matthew 1:21 that before the first Christmas day, the angel of the Lord appeared to Joseph, Mary's fiancee, and informed him that Mary "will bear a Son; and you shall call His name Jesus, for it is He who will save His people from their sins" (NASB). Upon reading that, we might say to ourselves, "But they didn't call Him Immanuel, they called Him Jesus!" And at first there seems to be a conflict, but that is really not the case. As Matthew continues to reveal in the next verses of his Gospel:

> Now all this took place that what was spoken by the Lord through the prophet might be fulfilled, saying, "Behold the virgin shall be with child, and shall bear a Son, and they shall call His name Immanuel," which translated means, "God with us" (Matthew 1:22-23 NASB).

Often in the Bible, names communicate character. The name Immanuel, or "God with us," speaks of the mysterious union of the divine and the human which has historically been found only once—in the person of Christ. It tells us that Christ was the God-man, a portion of the Trinity—God the Son, veiled in flesh. Christ was (and is) God, and Christ was (and is) man. The very fact that He was miraculously born of a virgin qualified Him to be "God with us," and fulfilled the promise of His name. In the words of Colossians 2:9, "For in Christ all the fullness of the Deity lives in bodily form" (NIV). By His very nature and character He was Immanuel.

The earthly name attached to our Savior, Jesus, means "Jehovah [God], the Savior," or "the salvation of Jehovah." This, Christ's human name, speaks of the mission that He came to perform while upon the earth. As Paul writes in Philippians 2:7, Christ Jesus "emptied Himself, taking the form of a bond-servant, and being made in the likeness of men. And being found in appearance as a man, He humbled Himself by becoming obedient to the point of death, even death on a cross" (NASB). That was His mission, and because of His death, in which He bore our sins, we through faith may be clothed in His righteousness. The salvation of the Lord can truly be ours . . . all because nearly 2000 years ago our Savior walked in the midst of humankind as "God with us."

OF SIGNS TO COME

Isaiah's prediction, recorded in chapter 7, verse 14, of his book, has been totally fulfilled in Jesus Christ. The same cannot yet be said for the next prophecy we will consider. Does that mean that God's Word is inaccurate? Certainly not! Rather, part of the fulfillment of the next prophecy remains to be seen, and may well come to pass within the span of our own lifetimes. In Isaiah 9:6-7, we read:

> For a child will be born to us, a son will be given to us;
> And the government will rest on His shoulders;
> And His name will be called Wonderful Counselor, Mighty God,
> Eternal Father, Prince of Peace.
> There will be no end to the increase of His government or of peace,
> On the throne of David and over his kingdom,
> To establish it and to uphold it with justice and righteousness
> From then on and forevermore.
> The zeal of the LORD of hosts will accomplish this (NASB).

MORE OF THE CHILD

"For a child will be born to us, a son will be given to us," the prophet first exclaims. The word *child* speaks of Christ's humanity—He was born (though not conceived) like any other human being; the label *son* reminds us of His deity— He was the Son of God, given to us by His heavenly Father. The term *us* refers to the nation of Israel, the people chosen to receive Him.

The powerful words of John 3:16 tell us, "For God so loved the world, that He gave His only begotten Son, that whoever believes in Him should not perish, but have eternal life" (NASB). This was an act of Almighty God, sending His own Son, in human flesh, in literal fulfillment of Isaiah's prophecy given centuries earlier. God's purpose was to purchase man's redemption through the shedding of this Son's blood. In the words of Romans 6:23, "For the wages of sin is death, but the free gift of God is eternal life in Christ Jesus our Lord" (NASB). In view of this amazing truth, how can we not proclaim this Christmas, with the apostle Paul, "Thanks be to God for His indescribable gift" (2 Corinthians 9:15 NASB)? It is a gift too wonderful for words.

HIS RANK

But there is more to Isaiah's prophecy. Not only was a Son to be born, but "the government will rest on His shoulders" (9:6). What exactly does this mean? Does this speak of a time when Christ will carry the whole weight of the world upon His shoulders, bearing it as a crushing burden? I don't believe so. Instead, I contend that the picture in Isaiah 9:6 is one of victory.

In ancient days, men who were in authority wore regal robes draped across their shoulders which symbolized their positions. We observe a similar practice today. Any military man will tell you that bars on the shoulders of a soldier signify the rank of captain, and leaves represent the rank of major. Full colonels wear eagles on their shoulders, and generals sport stars.

When I read that the government of the world will rest upon the shoulders of Christ, a vivid picture comes to mind of Revelation 19:16, where the apostle John recounts the vision given him of Jesus' second coming. John describes Christ as astride a white horse, His eyes aflame, His head crowned with many diadems, His body clothed in a robe dipped in blood. Writes the apostle in verse 16, "And on His robe and on His thigh He has a name written, 'King of kings, and Lord of lords'" (NASB). What a glorious portrait! Someday we shall see that name—denoting the rank of King of kings—emblazoned across the robe and thigh of Christ, as He comes finally to set up the kingdom described in Isaiah 9:6-7. Because of His nature and attributes, the government of the earth will not be a difficult burden for Him. He will rule in truth and reign with righteousness forever and ever!

As John puts it in Revelation 19:6, "Hallelujah! For the Lord our God, the Almighty, reigns" (NASB).

His Titles

It is interesting that in Matthew 2:2, we read that the magi or wise men from the east, seeking the Christ child, followed the star to Jerusalem and asked the question, "Where is He who has been born King of the Jews?" (NASB). Though men from another culture might recognize His royalty, during His earthly ministry Jesus would not be accepted as "King of the Jews" by the majority of His own people. At some point in the future, perhaps very soon, He will return again to establish His everlasting kingdom.

At that time, Isaiah tells us, Christ will be called by several titles: "Wonderful Counselor, Mighty God, Eternal Father, Prince of Peace" (9:6). These four designations describe His character. He is worthy of each name even now.

Wonderful Counselor. How aptly this name describes Christ. He is the wonderful counselor. Nobody does it better! As Paul tells the Roman Christians in Romans 11:34, "Who has known the mind of the Lord? Or who has been his counselor?" (NIV). None have counseled the Lord, for He is all-knowing. He offers wisdom and advice to those who peruse the sacred page of Scripture to find direction for their lives. He waits to do the same for any of us who truly seek to know Him more intimately.

Mighty God. Christ is also God almighty, who keeps His promises and who has the power and strength to fulfill the words of His mouth. Nothing is impossible with Him! As He revealed to the prophet Jeremiah, "Behold, I am the LORD, the God of all flesh; is anything too difficult for Me?" (Jeremiah 32:27 NASB).

Eternal Father. Not only is Christ the wonderful counselor and mighty God, but He is the eternal Father. That concept can be hard to grasp, but let's remember that we worship a God who is three-in-one. He is an all-powerful, co-existing Trinity: God the Father, God the Son, and God the Spirit, present from before the foundation of the world.

In the upper room, when Christ was sharing a final meal with His disciples before His crucifixion, Philip said to Him, "Lord, show us the Father, and it is enough for us" (John 14:8 NASB). Jesus, perhaps hurt, certainly disappointed, looked into Philip's face and made this reply: "Have I been so long with you, and yet you have not come to know Me, Philip? He who has seen Me has seen the Father; how do you say, 'Show us the Father'?" (John 14:9 NASB).

What Philip couldn't fathom was that God Himself reclined at the same table with him, sharing the same food and drink! The apostle John begins his Gospel with this remarkable description of Jesus Christ:

> In the beginning was the Word, and the Word was with God, and the Word was God. He was in the beginning with God. All things came into being by Him, and apart from Him nothing came into being that has come into being (John 1:1-3 NASB; see also Colossians 1:6).

A few verses later, John tells us of this Word, "And the Word became flesh, and dwelt among us, and we beheld His glory, glory as of the only begotten from the Father, full of grace and truth" (1:14 NASB). The Word-become-flesh is none other than Jesus Christ. As the final verse of the beloved Christmas carol goes:

> Yea, Lord, we greet Thee, Born this happy morning,
> Jesus, to Thee be all glory given;

Word of the Father, Now in flesh appearing,
O come, let us adore Him, O come let us adore Him,
O come, let us adore Him, Christ the Lord.

> (Frederick Oakeley, trans.
> "O Come All Ye Faithful")

Prince of Peace. Finally, Isaiah calls Christ the prince of peace. How well that defines His character! To His children, He brings *upward, inward,* and *outward* peace.

The *upward peace* comes when we are reconciled to God by receiving Jesus Christ as Savior. In the words of Paul in Romans 5:1-2:

> Therefore, since we have been justified through faith, we have peace with God through our Lord Jesus Christ, through whom we have gained access by faith into this grace in which we now stand. And we rejoice in the hope of the glory of God (NIV).

The *inward peace* comes to the believer as he surrenders himself—his hopes, thoughts, ambitions, trials, and fears—to the Lord. In Philippians 4, Paul teaches the Christians at Philippi that if they rejoice always in the Lord, declining to be anxious but rather trusting Him and making their requests known to Him through prayer, then "the peace of God, which surpasses all comprehension, shall guard your hearts and your minds in Christ Jesus" (Philippians 4:7 NASB; see also 4:4-6). That is a tremendous promise to us as well. Everything is going to be all right because our Father has us in His hands.

The Lord is the bringer of *outward peace,* too. He is able to make even our enemies to be at peace with us. As Proverbs 16:7 puts it, "When a man's ways are pleasing to the LORD, He makes even his enemies to be at peace with him"

(NASB). And eventually, Christ will reign over a world which will be completely at peace.

HIS GOVERNMENT

If you stop to think about it, the final statement in the paragraph above is quite remarkable. In our country today, we have peace marches and peace movements. We are urged to support nuclear freezes and diplomatic thaws. War protesters picket nuclear missile silos and stage sit-ins at the gates of military bases to show their loathing of armed conflict. Contributors by the thousands mail checks to organizations purporting to work for world peace. Ironically, however, there is only one individual capable of ensuring a world of harmony—a world without hunger, violence, crime, and war. That person is, of course, the prince of peace, Jesus Christ. As verse 7 of Isaiah 9 goes on to say of Him:

> There will be no end to the increase of His government or of peace,
> On the throne of David and over his kingdom,
> To establish it and to uphold it with justice and righteousness
> From then on and forevermore.
> The zeal of the Lord of hosts will accomplish this (NASB).

It will be at some future point that the Christ, the Son of the living God, will usher in the eternal kingdom described in the passage above. Luke 1:32-33 reveals that in that day, Christ:

> . . . will be great, and will be called the Son of the Most High; and the Lord God will give Him the throne of His

father David; and He will reign over the house of Jacob forever; and His kingdom will have no end (NASB).

His Zeal

What will bring about this fantastic reign? As Isaiah reveals, nothing but the "zeal of the LORD of hosts" (9:7) will be able to accomplish this. The Lord's zeal—His fervor, ardor, and passion—is seen many times in Scripture. Frequently when the word *zeal* appears, it is preceded by a judgment of some sort. For example, in John 2:13-16, we read of Jesus' trip to Jerusalem at Passover time. Finding the temple brimming with merchants and moneychangers, He fashioned a whip of cords and drove them from the premises, scattering coins and overturning tables. It was an act of divine judgment against those who had turned a sacred place into a den of commerce. John 2:17 says when the disciples saw what Christ had done, they "remembered that it was written, 'Zeal for Thy house will consume me'" (NASB).

Every time we read of judgment in the book of Revelation, we must realize that it is going to be the zeal of the Lord which will bring forth this judgment. Once this occurs, Christ's kingdom will be ushered in. In the meantime, we pray what Jesus taught His disciples in the Lord's Prayer: "Thy kingdom come. Thy will be done, On earth as it is in heaven" (Matthew 6:10 NASB).

But the reality of God's judgment is not to be forgotten, shoved into the dark recesses of our minds. According to Revelation 1:18, Christ holds the keys to death and Hades. His judgment of nonbelievers is a coming reality, stirringly expressed in the strains of the immortal "Battle Hymn of the Republic":

Mine eyes have seen the glory of the coming of the Lord;

He is trampling out the vintage where the grapes of
wrath are stored;
He hath loosed the fateful lightening of His terrible
swift sword;
His truth is marching on.

(Julia Ward Howe)

JEREMIAH—THE PRESENT AND COMING RIGHTEOUSNESS

Yes, Christ is coming again. He is coming as a King to
reign eternally, and to sit upon the throne of His father,
David. We learn that from Isaiah's prophecy.

Yet Isaiah is not the only Old Testament writer to have
made this prediction. Jeremiah also spoke similar words.

The priest Jeremiah lived and prophecied some one hundred years after Isaiah. His prophetic ministry began in 626
B.C., and continued for forty years. The book of Scripture
bearing his name contains a blistering denunciation of the
idolatry and blatant sin practiced by his countrymen. Tearful-
ly, Jeremiah predicted the downfall of the nation of Judah,
and her seventy-year Babylonian captivity, yet not without
calling for the people to repent.

But even though the weeping prophet's writings overflow
with warnings of impending doom, there are also flashes of
hope, promises of a better day. One of these is found in
Jeremiah 23:5-6, where we read:

"The days are coming," declares the LORD,
    "when I will raise up to David a righteous Branch,
a King who will reign wisely
    and do what is just and right in the land.
In His days Judah will be saved
    and Israel will live in safety.
This is the name by which he will be called:
    The LORD Our Righteousness" (NIV).

Remember that in 2 Samuel 7:13, the Lord spoke to David, promising him that one of his descendants would sit upon the throne of an eternal kingdom. This "greater son" will establish David's kingdom forever and ever. That person is the "righteous Branch" spoken of by Jeremiah in verse 5, chapter 23, of his book. We know Him as Jesus Christ.

When we think of a branch in genealogy, we think of it in relation to a family tree. The branch mentioned by Jeremiah springs forth from the earthly family tree of King David, and the heavenly family of God. As Isaiah 11:1 tells us, "A shoot will come up from the stump of Jesse [David's father]; from his roots a Branch will bear fruit" (NIV). This branch will be far more than a human descendant; one glorious day He will be "a King who will reign wisely and do what is just and right in the land" (Jeremiah 23:5 NIV). Later in his book, Jeremiah similarly writes that this "Branch . . . shall execute justice and righteousness on the earth" (Jeremiah 33:15 NASB). He will judge; He will reign with complete wisdom and goodness. As Isaiah 4:2 tells us, "In that day, the Branch of the LORD will be beautiful and glorious, and the fruit of the earth will be the pride and the adornment of the survivors of Israel" (NASB).

In the tremendous age when His kingdom is finally established throughout the world, this branch, Jesus Christ, will be called by a special name: "The LORD Our Righteousness" (Jeremiah 23:6). What a glorious future is planned and prepared for those who belong to Him. Christ's will indeed be a rule and reign of righteousness!

We men, women, and children have no righteousness of our own. Cautions the prophet Isaiah, "All of us have become like one who is unclean, and all our righteous acts are like filthy rags; we all shrivel up like a leaf, and like the wind our sins sweep us away" (Isaiah 64:6 NIV). Christ must become our righteousness, or we'll never walk through the gates of heaven! Acceptance of His righteousness involves an act of will on our part, in which we commit ourselves to Him by faith. This is the gospel, the good news of Christ. Writes the apostle Paul in Romans 1:16-17:

> For I am not ashamed of the gospel, for it is the power of God for salvation to everyone who believes, to the Jew first and also to the Greek. For in it the righteousness of God is revealed from faith to faith; as it is written, "But the righteous man shall live by faith" (NASB).

We must clothe ourselves in righteousness other than that of our own making, choosing the glorious raiment of God rather than the "filthy rags" of man. We must allow the One who will be called "The LORD Our Righteousness" to cleanse and redeem us. We must believe as does this hymnwriter:

> My hope is built on nothing less
> Than Jesus' blood and righteousness;
> I dare not trust the sweetest frame,
> But wholly lean on Jesus' name.
> On Christ, the solid Rock, I stand;
> All other ground is sinking sand,
> All other ground is sinking sand.
>
> (Edward Motes, "The Solid Rock")

The ground around us is but sinking sand . . . until we grasp the branch of Christ in firm belief. Then we shall have unwrapped the most beautiful and timeless of presents, as we receive the gift of the salvation of God through Jesus. Dressed in His righteousness alone, we shall stand without fault before the throne! (See Jude 24,25.)

MICAH—HONOR COMES TO THE LEAST OF ALL

During the days of Isaiah, a simple villager also uttered the most profound of prophecies. His name was Micah, and theologians classify him as one of the "minor prophets" of the Old Testament. From the pen of this contemporary of Isaiah came a remarkable prediction concerning the birth of the righteous branch, Jesus Christ. The word of the Lord came to Micah, saying:

> But you, Bethlehem Ephrathah,
>   though you are small among the clans of
>   Judah,
> out of you will come for me
>   one who will be ruler over Israel,
> whose origins are from old,
>   from ancient times (Micah 5:2 NIV).

The name *Bethlehem* means "house of bread"; *Ephrathah* is defined as "the fruit fields," or "the fertile ones." The names refer to the same small town, a tiny village about five miles from Jerusalem. According to Micah, it would be from this seemingly unimportant locale that a great ruler—the Messiah Himself—would emerge. And anyone in the prophet's day who was willing to listen would have known about the location of delivery 750 years before the fact.

You wouldn't think that God would choose to send the Savior of the world to the middle-eastern equivalent of what we Texans would call "a one-horse town." Surely God would choose the nearby metropolis of Jerusalem as the Messiah's birthplace! And certainly Christ would make a spectacular, splashy entrance into the arena of human life—landing at the city of Zion, splitting the Mount of Olives on the way down, so that everyone would recognize Him as King!

But Christ didn't come that way. Instead He was born in a little place, a small village, a miniscule dot on the road map. If you blinked when driving through Bethlehem, you'd have missed it! True, it was fairly well known as the place toward which Jacob and company were journeying when Rachel, the patriarch's much-loved wife, died and was buried (see Genesis

35:19). And Bethlehem was the home of Jesse and the birth-place of David. But it was still a little town.

That tells me something. God doesn't overlook the little places. The "little town of Bethlehem" which we sing about at Christmas was relatively insignificant in the eyes of the people of Micah's era. It was unimportant 750 years later, too . . . until the Lord chose to come there. Then it was never the same again. Luke 2:1-7 tells us:

> In those days Caesar Augustus issued a decree that a census should be taken of the entire Roman world. . . . And everyone went to his own town to register.
>
> So Joseph also went up from the town of Nazareth in Galilee to Judea, to Bethlehem, the town of David, be-cause he belonged to the house and line of David. He went there to register with Mary, who was pledged to be married to him, and was expecting a child. While they were there, the time came for the baby to be born, and she gave birth to her firstborn, a son. She wrapped him in cloths and placed him in a manger, because there was no room for them in the inn (NIV).

How incredibly the Lord works to fulfill His plans and purposes! He prompted an emperor to call for a census. This forced Joseph to make a journey to the town of his ancestor, David. Required to bring his wife, Joseph couldn't say to Mary, "Honey, you stay at home at Nazareth, and I'll run down to Bethlehem and pay the taxes." Instead, the very pregnant young woman had to accompany her husband on a trip rugged and rough enough to make any modern obstetri-cian scream with alarm. It was the law . . . but God also needed Mary in Bethlehem for the birthday of a King, her firstborn son—the "ruler over Israel," who, because He is God, has "origins . . . from old, from ancient times" (Micah 5:2).

We can but marvel at the humble circumstances in which

God came to dwell among us. And too, how gracious it was of God to reveal the front-page news about little Bethelem's coming glory to a simple, unassuming villager named Micah. God always does the exceeding, the abundant, and the unexpected!

ZECHARIAH—THE LIFE OF THE KING

If Micah tells us about the lowly situation into which our Lord was born, the prophet Zechariah gives us glimpses of the humility that characterized His life on earth. Zechariah was born during the Babylonian captivity which Jeremiah had so vigorously warned his people would occur. To place things historically, the dire warnings of Jeremiah were uttered some 100 years before Zechariah would begin his own prophetic ministry; Isaiah and Micah had preached 230 years before Zechariah.

Compared to the other three men we have considered, Zechariah lived closest to the time of the first coming of Christ, but even so, he still made his predictions over 500 years before Jesus would walk the earth. More than five centuries before it would ever happen, the prophet was able to exclaim:

> Rejoice greatly, O Daughter of Zion!
>   Shout, Daughter of Jerusalem!
> See, your king comes to you,
>   righteous and having salvation,
>   gentle and riding on a donkey,
>   on a colt, the foal of a donkey
>   (Zechariah 9:9 NIV).

The babe who was born at Bethlehem grew to manhood and began His public ministry. Empowered by the Holy Spirit, for three years He preached and taught, prayed and performed miracles. He healed the blind, the lame, the terminally ill. He raised two people from the dead and He wept with compassion at the desperation of the masses. He spent time with those usually overlooked or even shunned by society: small children, tax collectors, prostitutes. He freely gave of Himself to the twelve common men He had chosen as disciples. None were insignificant or beyond hope—to Him.

A week before He was to die upon the cross of Calvary, He entered the city of Jerusalem through its eastern gate. His mount was neither a magnificent stallion nor even a sturdy camel. He rode upon a donkey borrowed from a nearby village.

Matthew 21 tells us that throngs of people walked in front of Him, while crowds followed behind. Branches from trees were cut and strewn across His path, a carpet of green marking His way. The cries of the parading multitudes rose in fevered pitch:

> Hosanna to the Son of David;
> Blessed is He who comes in the name of the Lord;
> Hosanna in the highest! (Matthew 21:9 NASB).

And thus what was spoken through the prophet in Zechariah 9:9 was fulfilled.

POINTS TO PONDER

Zechariah's prediction makes mention of five qualities describing Christ which are worthy of special note. He tells us of Jesus' *kingship,* His *righteousness,* His *salvation,* His *gentleness,* and His *humility.* Let's consider these briefly.

The prophet, like so many before him, speaks of Christ as "righteous." His revelation agrees with the other predictions we have studied. Christ, the God-man, is totally righteous, completely just, and free from blemish.

Zechariah also states that the King upon the donkey is "having salvation." As we have mentioned earlier, Christ offers us His salvation. It is a gift available whenever we choose to believe and accept it. Acts 4:12 tells us of Jesus Christ, "And there is salvation in no one else; for there is no other name under heaven that has been given among men, by which we must be saved" (NASB).

Third, note that Zechariah describes Christ as "gentle." Some people are too scared to come to God. It's as if they believe the bumper sticker I saw the other day which read: "God is back, and boy is He mad!" But God isn't like that. Rather, the arms of God are always extended, expressing the longing He feels for reconciliation with us.

In fact, the Lord Jesus is very gentle. John 8:3-11 tells the story of a woman who has been caught in the act of adultery. Tears redden her eyes and stain her face as she is brought to Christ. A condemning crowd gathers round, eager to crush her with stones for her crime. Does Jesus order her execution? No. Instead He speaks to her accusers, "He who is without sin among you, let him be the first to throw a stone at her" (John 8:7 NASB). One by one the people leave, disappearing like termites into the woodwork. Not one stone is cast.

"Woman," asks the Lord, "where are they? Did no one condemn you?"

"No one, Lord," comes her reply.

"Neither do I condemn you; go your way. From now on sin no more," responds Jesus in gentleness and mercy (John 8:10-11 NASB). He is like that—approachable, kind, forgiving.

And, as Zechariah also reveals, He is humble. The Lord of all the universe chose to ride into His capital city upon a simple donkey. He could have commanded the angelic host to escort Him that Palm Sunday. He could have ordered a flaming chariot from heaven drawn by fiery horses for His conveyance. But He didn't. Instead He chose to present Himself to us in all humility, even as He was born in the manger of a stable. In Matthew 11:28-29, Jesus is quoted as saying:

> Come to Me, all who are weary and heavy
> laden, and I will give you rest.
> Take My yoke upon you, and learn from Me,
> for I am gentle and humble in heart; and you shall
> find rest for your souls (NASB).

Christ is the righteous Savior. He is gentle and humble. But He is also a King, as Zechariah calls Him. The wise men searched for the newborn King, but His own people overlooked Him. Some thirty-three years later, as He hung upon the cross, the witnesses to His suffering placed a sign above His head which sarcastically read, "This is Jesus the king of the Jews" (Matthew 27:37).

You see, the waiting world didn't expect Him to come the first time in such lowly circumstances. They didn't expect the Messiah to be a suffering servant, but a conquering monarch. And such He will be upon His return to our midst.

Jesus Is Coming Again

Zechariah 12:10 proclaims the words of the Lord to the prophet:

> And I will pour out on the house of David and on the inhabitants of Jerusalem, the Spirit of grace and of supplication, so that they will look on Me whom they have pierced; and they will mourn for Him, as one mourns for an only son, and they will weep bitterly over Him, like the bitter weeping over a first-born (NASB).

At Christ's second coming every eye will behold Him. All will look upon the One who was pierced for us, as He triumphantly returns—the conquering King of kings. Revelation 1:7 says:

> Behold, He is coming with the clouds, and every eye will see Him, even those who pierced Him; and all the tribes of the earth will mourn over Him. Even so. Amen (NASB).

That is how it will be. Yet before that dramatic re-entry, those of us who are Christians will have already joined Him in the clouds. Writes the apostle Paul in 1 Thessalonians 4:16-17:

> For the Lord Himself will descend from heaven with a shout, with the voice of the archangel, and with the trumpet of God; and the dead in Christ shall rise first. Then we who are alive and remain shall be caught up together with them in the clouds to meet the Lord in the air, and thus we shall always be with the Lord (NASB, see also 1 Corinthians 15:51-54).

This prophetic event, known as the rapture of the church, could occur at any moment. Nothing stands in the way scripturally of the instantaneous fulfillment of this promise. It might happen today! To paraphrase Amos 4:12, we should prepare to meet our God.

Hundreds of years before the first Christmas, God revealed to man that Christ would be born of a virgin in the small city of Bethlehem. He would be a descendant of David—the Son of God coming in the form of a little child. And it all happened. How then can we doubt that the rapture and His triumphal second coming will take place just as God's Word says it will? We'd better be ready. We have already been warned.

IGNORING THE OBVIOUS

People tend to ignore even the most blatant of warnings, don't they? I remember my years working in Christian camping in the northwest. During ski season, the threat of avalanches was ever present, posing a very real danger.

When heavy snowfall accumulates on a mountain ledge, a cornice is often formed. When skiiers swoosh across the top, the packed snow, under pressure, can easily give way and bury any who are underneath. In the northwest, as a precaution following each snowfall, forest service personnel rope off dangerous areas, marking them clearly as possible avalanche sites. Once this is done, the government staff at the mountain travels to each prohibited location. Since sharp noises can also trigger avalanches, they fire artillery shells into the packed snow, hoping to send the tons of white stuff crashing down, removing the danger of uncontrolled avalanche. Only then are the warning ropes barricading the area removed.

Despite the fact that a section may be marked off as dangerous, many times skiers ignore the warnings. Unskiied snow is every skier's thrill, and, tempted by the fresh powder, they venture, undaunted by the danger, into avalanche areas. Certain of their own invincibility, numerous skiiers decide it is worth the risk to make their own fresh tracks in the newfallen snow. Besides, an avalanche won't really happen, will it?

Usually, it doesn't. But I recall one horrifying instance when it did. Six Canadians, who had come down to the States for a day's skiing, sped through the forest service warning barriers out into the inviting powdery whiteness. This proved to be their last great act of defiance. Shortly thereafter, they were buried under an immense wall of snow and ice in the worst avalanche in years. They must not have believed the warnings, or they'd never have tried the stunt which left them crushed beneath a mass of snow and ice. Did they have regrets in that last millisecond before their lives ended in the roar of the avalanche? Did they have time to think back to the ropes which had signified impending danger? Did they wish they had paid attention to the signs? I imagine they did.

Let's not let the same thing be said of us regarding the warnings in Scripture.

Not to Be Overlooked

Following the rapture and a seven-year period of tribulation, Christ will return, bringing judgment first (Revelation 6–19). Then He will set up His kingdom (Revelation 20). Daniel 7:13-14 tells us that He will come at night in the clouds of heaven. Zechariah 14:4-9 reveals that His feet will touch the Mount of Olives, splitting it asunder, and that this will happen on a unique day, known only to God. Revelation 22:20 says of Christ, "He who testifies to these things says, 'Yes, I am coming quickly'" (NASB). The apostle John echoes the thoughts of every Christian who waits in eager anticipation for the rapture of the church: "Amen. Come, Lord Jesus" (Revelation 22:20 NASB).

King Herod wasn't prepared for the first coming of Christ. Matthew 2 tells us that when the wise men from the east came to Jerusalem looking for the child, Herod was perplexed. He gathered the chief priests and scribes, who told him that Bethlehem was to be the location of the birth. He tried to trick the magi into returning to Jerusalem and revealing the exact whereabouts of the Christ child. He was not ready or willing to accept the coming of the King, and he fought against Christ with every ounce of his energy.

So What Are You Doing about It?

Are you fighting against Christ? Or are you passively resisting giving yourself to Him? Examine yourself. Have you asked Jesus into your heart as Savior? Have you yielded yourself to Him so that He might be Lord of your life? If you have never done it before, or if you have drifted away from the Sovereign, I invite you to consider the Christchild this Christmas. He is waiting for you to respond. His words recorded in Revelation 3:20 vividly present His open invitation to all who desire a relationship with Him:

> Behold, I stand at the door and knock; if anyone hears My voice and opens the door, I will come in to him, and will dine with him, and he with Me (NASB).

The rapture could happen this Christmas. Would you be caught up in the clouds? Or would you be among those standing startled on the ground, muttering, "I wish we'd all been ready"?

Printed on a Christmas card which Pearl and I received last December was this imaginative poem, "'Twas the Night before Jesus Came," which describes what your Christmas could be like if the rapture should occur before you have made proper preparations. Believe me, it wouldn't be the holiday you had in mind.

> 'Twas the night before Jesus came and all through
>   the house
>   Not a creature was praying, not one in the house.
> Their Bibles were lain on the shelf without care
>   In hopes that Jesus would not come there.
>
> The children were dressing to crawl into bed,
>   Not once ever kneeling or bowing a head.
> And mom in her rocker with baby on her lap
>   Was watching the Late Show while I took a nap.
>
> When out of the East there arose such a clatter,
>   I sprang to my feet to see what was the matter.

Away to the window I flew like a flash
   Tore open the shutters and threw up the sash!

When what to my wondering eyes should appear
   But angels proclaiming that Jesus was here.
With a light like the sun sending forth a bright ray
   I knew in a moment this must be THE DAY!

The light of His face made me cover my head
   It was Jesus! returning just like He had said.
And though I possessed worldly wisdom and wealth,
   I cried when I saw Him in spite of myself.

In the Book of Life which He held in His hand
   Was written the name of every saved man.
He spoke not a word as He searched for my name;
   When He said, "It's not here," my head hung in
      shame.

The people whose names had been written with love
   He gathered to take to His Father above.
With those who were ready He rose without a sound
   While all the rest were left standing around.

I fell to my knees, but it was too late;
   I had waited too long and thus sealed my fate.
I stood and I cried as they rose out of sight;
   Oh, if only I had been ready tonight.

In the words of this poem the meaning is clear;
   The coming of Jesus is drawing near.
There's only one life and when comes this last call
   We'll find that the Bible was true after all!

                           (Author unknown)

Reflections for the season

1. Christ is the rope of life binding together the Bible.

2. He is Immanuel, "God with us."

3. Jesus is the wonderful counselor, the mighty God, the eternal Father, and the Prince of peace.

4. The rapture may happen today! Are you ready?

A Voice in the Wilderness
Luke 1:5-80

*I*n many families, Christmas is the time for elaborate gift-giving. Among certain clusters of relatives, the holiday turns into a sort of competition—a giant spectacle of oneupsmanship in which siblings and other family members vie for the honor of giving the best, the biggest, the fanciest present. You know the story. Uncle Gerry buys Grandma Turner a microwave, so Aunt Dotty springs for a new color TV. Not to be outdone, Aunt Freda and Uncle Charlie join forces to purchase Gram a new Oldsmobile, while cousin Alfred settles for buying her a gift certificate to Tiffany's. All that . . . when what Grandma would really like is just a new nightgown and a subscription to the large-print version of *Reader's Digest!*

A MATTER OF PRIDE

One particular family I know, on a rather tight budget, gives modest, yet respectably nice Christmas presents. The other side of the same family is known for overdoing the season, running up charge cards to the limit with expensive buys. The less extravagant bunch feels a bit intimidated by the flashier folks. Each holiday celebration brings with it a host of comparisons and leaves the slight aftertaste of embarrassment with the more modest group. You see, it's a matter of pride.

Pride is a dangerous thing. The instrument of pride is one of the prime tools Satan can use to subtly work his desires upon mankind. He uses pride to keep us out of the family of God by convincing us that, with our good deeds, we can earn our way into heaven. When we do become part of God's family, Satan may also use pride to cause us to want to do things our way, instead of the Lord's way. Thus we remain fleshly or carnal, never becoming grown-up Christians.

Surprisingly, Satan can also use pride to interfere with the growth of even those we think of as extremely mature Christians. I'm talking about the super-spiritual saints who have lived so long with the Lord that they've ceased to be teachable. Their pride focuses on the level of their spiritual maturity. Often they'll remark to a preacher that the sermon was too basic, or meant for someone else. They'll say that they need more of the "meat of the Word." When I hear consistent comments like those from another Christian, I begin to suspect that maybe the needle on his pride gauge has shot off the dial. No matter who we are, or how long we have known God through Jesus Christ, we are all vulnerable to the temptation of pride.

During Christmas, it's pride which causes us to overspend so that we can keep up with the Joneses or the Aunt Fredas and Uncle Charlies. It's pride which burns a smouldering hole of bitter regret when finances don't enable us to lavish those we love with expensive do-dads. And it's pride which may well ruin our celebration of the season when we focus on what we don't have and can't do, rather than on what we do have and can do, and on what Jesus Christ has done for us!

THE SOLUTION?

What is the solution to pride? The answer lies in letting God work in us to create an attitude of humility. Charles Haddon Spurgeon once said, "Humility is to make a right estimate of one's self." Being humble means seeing ourselves as we really are. How do we make that "right estimate" of ourselves? I'm not sure of the identity of the writer of this poem, but he surely offers a terrific suggestion on the subject:

Sometime when you're feeling important,
Sometime when your ego's way up,
Sometime when you take it for granted
That you are the prize-winning pup;
Sometime when you feel that your absence
Would leave an unfillable hole,
Just follow these simple instructions
And see how it humbles your soul:

Take a bucket and fill it with water,
Put your hand in it up to your wrist,
Now pull it out fast and the hole that remains
Is the measure of how you'll be missed.

You may splash all you please as you enter,
And stir up the water galore,
But stop and you'll find in a minute
It's back where it was before.

The essence of humility is realizing that there are none irreplaceable, none indispensable. While we're on earth, we may make waves and stir up the waters as we splish and splash. We may influence people and spur them to action. But in the end, what we've done apart from God won't count all that much (see Psalm 75:6-7). And we'll find that a healthy dose of humility along the way would have prevented us from seeing ourselves as too important.

The Word of God exhorts us to such humility in several places. For example, the apostle Peter urges his readers, "Humble yourselves therefore under the mighty hand of God, that he may exalt you in due time" (1 Peter 5:6 KJV). And Paul implores the Philippian Christians:

> Do nothing from selfishness or empty conceit, but with humility of mind let each of you regard one another as more important than himself; do not merely look out for your own personal interests, but also for the interests of others (Philippians 2:3-4 NASB).

The apostle also writes these words to the believers in Rome:

> For by the grace given me I say to every one of you: Do not think of yourself more highly than you ought, but rather think of yourself with sober judgment, in accordance with the measure of faith God has given you (Romans 12:3 NIV).

JOHN: THE EPITOME OF HUMILITY

God's Word gives us a prime example of a man who, throughout the course of his entire life, possessed a "right estimate" of himself. He epitomized humility. He knew that his role in life would be essentially secondary, and he performed his God-given tasks very successfully. He was John the Baptist.

When Christ began His earthly ministry, John's followers drifted away to join Him. When his disciples questioned John about his apparent loss of influence, he calmly and simply explained that he had only been sent to bear witness to the coming of the Savior. He was not the bridegroom, but merely the friend of the bridegroom. Without a shred of regret or an ounce of envy, John looked the disciples squarely in the eye and said this of Christ, "He must be continually increasing, and I must be continually decreasing" (John 3:30, see also John 3:26-31). What a refreshing—and convicting—expression of humility!

It will be our pleasure and privilege to consider the circumstances surrounding the birth of this messenger whose purpose in life was to herald the coming of the Messiah. As we do so, we'll be examining Luke 1:5-80. Unless otherwise indicated, the Scripture references given are taken from my personal translation of the Greek text.

As the beautiful story in the Gospel of Luke unfolds, it is my prayer that we shall rejoice as we witness the godly beginnings of the one whom Isaiah the prophet referred to when he wrote these words over seven hundred years before John's birthday:

> A voice is calling,
> "Clear the way for the LORD in the wilderness;
> Make smooth in the desert a highway for our God"
> (Isaiah 40:3 NASB).

Let's turn now to Scripture and meet the one destined to be a "voice" in the wilderness, clearing the way for the Lord Jesus Christ.

THE PLEASED PARENTS—LUKE 1:5-7

Luke 1:5 tells us, "There was in the days of Herod, King of Judea, a certain priest named Zacharias, of the division of Abijah; and his wife was of the daughters of Aaron, and her name was Elizabeth." It was to this couple that John would be born.

Zacharias was a priest. This means that he was of the tribe of Levi. Centuries before, King David had divided the priesthood into twenty-four sections (see 1 Chronicles 24:7-19), and as Luke reveals, Zacharias served in the section of Abijah. His wife Elizabeth, a descendant of Aaron, also came from a very religious, priestly line. Their backgrounds were similar, and we can safely assume that theirs was a compatible, godly marriage.

The very names of Zacharias and Elizabeth suggest that they marched to the same tune. *Zacharias* means, "God remembers"; *Elizabeth,* "His oath." Put it all together, and you have, "God remembers His oath," which He surely did in the lives of these two, as we shall see.

We read more of this devoted couple in verse 6 of Luke 1: "And they were both righteous in the sight of God, ordering their lives blamelessly in all the commandments and requirements of the Lord." What a tremendous testimony! Man looks on the outward appearance; God looks on the heart. When He gazed upon Zacharias and Elizabeth, He saw that they were godly people. They were readers of the Word, and careful also to be doers of the Word. They applied the Lord's teachings to their lives and sought His will in all things.

This beautiful couple stepping onto centerstage of history had been entrusted with a trial: they were childless, "because Elizabeth was barren, and they both had gone far in their days" (Luke 1:7). Never in their long marriage had the noise of children resounded from their home. Elizabeth, like Sarah, Rebekah, and Rachel, had difficulty conceiving. And now the prospects of childbirth were dim indeed, because Zacharias and Elizabeth were old. If they lived today, they'd probably already be retired and ensconced in a recreational community where they'd have unlimited time for golf, bridge, and checkers.

That reminds me of an experience one of my pals related to me. My friend Clemmo tells the story of revisiting his old high school several decades after he walked the stage in cap and gown. Plastered across an entire wall near the front of the school were panoramic pictures of each graduating class, from the 1920's to the present. As Clemmo eyeballed the photos, up walked a young fellow of sixteen or so to gawk over my friend's shoulder.

"Mister, did you go to this school?" the kid asked.

"Yes, I did," replied Clemmo. Pointing to one of the pictures on the wall, he said, "This is my class. Can you pick me out?"

The young fellow took a look at Clemmo, then perused the picture. He glanced back at Clemmo, and stared once more at the photograph. After a few minutes, he turned to my friend and said with resignation, "No sir, I can't."

Clemmo reached up and indicated a figure in the middle of the photo. "I'm the guy right here."

"Boy, sir," said the kid, looking from the picture to the gray-haired gentlemen beside it, "time sure did make a mess of you, didn't it?"

I love that story! As Luke 1 opens, Zacharias and Elizabeth were probably feeling that time had made a mess of them, too. They were on a downhill slide physically. They still desired children, but their infertility had long been accepted. The reality of the pain of arthritis had replaced most thoughts of the pangs of childbirth. But God had other ideas.

GABRIEL PAYS A VISIT TO ZACHARIAS—LUKE 1:8-23

We read in Luke 1:8-9 of Zacharias:

> Now it came about, while he was performing his priestly service before God in the appointed order of his division,
>
> According to the custom of the priestly office, he was chosen by lot when he entered into the temple of the Lord to burn incense.

Remember that the priesthood to which Zacharias belonged had been organized into twenty-four divisions. Each group was in charge of the Lord's temple in Jerusalem for two weeks out of the year. It was the time for the eighth division, that of Abijah, to serve, so Zacharias was performing his two-week tour of duty at the tabernacle.

This was an occasion of special honor for Zacharias. We read in verse 9 that he was "chosen by lot when he entered into the temple of the Lord to burn incense." This meant that he would be permitted to walk beyond the inner court of the tabernacle, where the burnt offering was sacrificed. He would enter the holy place, passing by the seven-branch candlesticks and table of shewbread. There he would approach the altar of incense, the place of prayer. Directly behind this, shielded by a veil, was the holy of holies, where the ark of the Lord was kept.

It was 3:00 P.M., the normal hour for the evening sacrifice, and "all the multitude of the people were praying outside" (Luke 1:10), when Zacharias reverently approached the holy place. Scripture reveals that suddenly "there appeared to him an angel of the Lord standing on the right side of the altar of incense" (Luke 1:11). An astonished Zacharias looked up to see the angel Gabriel shimmering before him in all his glory. It was a startling but magnificent moment.

A New Revelation

It had been four hundred years since the Lord had last directly communicated with man. The message to be conveyed to Zacharias by Gabriel would be the first revelation of God since that given to the prophet Malachi, whose book marks the end of the Old Testament. Now, after four centuries, the Lord was again going to speak, this time through His angel.

When the supernatural touches the natural, people usually become scared. That's one reason people fear death—they know that soon they will touch the supernatural, and they're simply not ready. Zacharias was greatly frightened at Gabriel's coming. We read that he was "troubled," and that "fear fell upon him" (Luke 1:12). He literally shook in his sandals.

The angel was quick to calm the man's fears, however. "Stop fearing, Zacharias," Gabriel said reassuringly, "because your petition has been heard and your wife Elizabeth shall bear you a son and you shall call his name John" (Luke 1:13). What amazing news! In Genesis 25:21 we read that Isaac prayed with his wife Rebekah because she had been barren for twenty years. I'm sure that, since they were a godly couple, Zacharias and Elizabeth had also many times knelt beside their bed in earnest prayer about their heartfelt desire to have a child. Perhaps, since Zacharias had come before the altar of prayer in the temple, he was praying about this very personal need at the moment Gabriel made his appearance. This is a possibility, since the priest at the altar prayed for his own family as well as his nation. As the angel's promise so vividly and tangibly illustrates, man's *extremity* is the Lord's *opportunity*. God's delays are not His denials!

THE MISSION OF THE PROMISED CHILD

Gabriel went on to describe to Zacharias what this son would be like:

> And you will have joy and gladness, and many will be rejoicing at his birth.
> For he shall be great in the sight of the Lord, and he will drink no wine or liquor; and he will be filled with the Holy Spirit while yet in his mother's womb.
> And he will turn back many of the sons of Israel to the Lord their God.
> And he will go before his face in the spirit and power of Elijah, to turn the hearts of the fathers back to the children, and the disobedient to the attitude of the

righteous; to prepare for the Lord a people having been made ready (Luke 1:14-17).

The baby boy would bring great happiness and rejoicing to his parents and others. He would be filled with the Holy Spirit even while in his mother's womb. He would grow to be highly favored by the Lord, becoming especially consecrated to God through the taking of the Nazarite vow (see Numbers 6:1-21). Like Samson, John would never cut his hair, take strong drink, or defile himself by touching the dead. His life would be set apart in its purity for a very special purpose.

The earthly mission of John the Baptist was clearly spelled out by Gabriel in verses 16 and 17. John was to preach in the spirit of Elijah, preparing the people for the coming of the Lord. He would not be the Lord, but he would have the very specific ministry of readying men and women to meet their God. He would turn the hearts of many of the children of Israel back to their Lord. He would be the voice in the wilderness spoken of by the prophet in Isaiah 40:3. John's role would be secondary; he would eventually be eclipsed by Christ Himself, and he would willingly and graciously submit to this fate.

DOUBTS CREEP IN

Of all the people of Israel who should have believed Gabriel's message, Zacharias was certainly one. He was a priest, a man well-schooled in the Scriptures, a man who thoroughly knew the past record of God's sovereign, supernatural intervention into human history. And yet the question he voiced showed that he had his doubts.

"Whereby shall I know this?" asked Zacharias of the angel, "For I am an old man and my wife has advanced in her days" (Luke 1:18). In other words, how could God give two senior citizens a son? We shouldn't be too critical of Zacharias here, for the angel's news was incredible. Zacharias and

Elizabeth were past retirement age . . . and children just aren't born to geriatric parents! But with God, all things are possible.

Zacharias was keeping his eyes upon the natural, not the supernatural, even with the angel of God standing before him. He had so often prayed, "God, give me a son," and yet he gaped in disbelief and skepticism when the Lord declared that He had heard his petition, and promised to answer his prayer.

Sarah reacted in a similar way when she overheard the Lord telling her husband Abraham that they would have a child within a year. Genesis 18:12 reveals that Sarah, eavesdropping behind the tent flap, laughed to herself upon hearing God's promise of a child. She was postmenopausal, after all, and so she snickered in unbelief and surprise. But within a year she was bouncing Isaac upon her knee. Great is the Lord's faithfulness, despite our lack of faith!

THE PENALTY

Gabriel studied the face of the doubting Zacharias, and then spoke again: "I am Gabriel, the one who stands before God, and I was sent to speak to you and to bring to you this good news" (Luke 1:19). In other words, who do you think I am, Zacharias? I didn't expect this kind of a reception from you—a godly, religious leader in the land. I am Gabriel, from the very presence of the Lord, and I've come to give you good news!

Then Gabriel pronounced a penalty upon Zacharias for his unbelief. "And behold you shall be silent and not able to speak until the day these things come to be, because you believed not my words, which shall be fulfilled in their season," the angel proclaimed (Luke 1:20). Until sometime after John's birth, Zacharias would be rendered mute, unable to tell even his beloved wife about the fantastic work of God which would take place through their lives. He had used his tongue in the wrong way; now he would not be able to use it at all for many months.

Notice also that Gabriel says that the Lord's promises "shall be fulfilled in their season." God never makes a promise that He doesn't intend to fulfill. He utters no empty words or vain vows, but means precisely what He says. All we must do is respond to Him in faith.

Hebrews 11:1 states that "faith is the assurance of things hoped for, the conviction of things not seen" (NASB). Faith is belief in what we cannot see; it's placing our trust in a sovereign God with whom all things are possible. As Oswald Chambers so eloquently writes in *My Utmost for His Highest,* "Faith never knows where it is being led, but it loves and knows the One Who is leading" (Chambers 1935, 79). "And without faith," continues the writer of Hebrews, "it is impossible to please God, because anyone who comes to him must believe that he exists and that he rewards those who earnestly seek him" (Hebrews 11:6 NIV).

In the appropriate season, the Lord would do for Zacharias and Elizabeth exactly as He said He would. They would become the parents of a baby boy long after the natural time for such a birth. Truly, as Solomon writes of God centuries before, "He hath made every thing beautiful in his time" (Ecclesiastes 3:11a KJV). He always does.

The Miracle Continues

It was a very different Zacharias who at last emerged from the temple. The people marveled that he had stayed so long within the holy place, and then they gazed dumbfounded when he walked out into their midst, unable to speak. He beckoned to the waiting crowds, making signs, but not one word issued from his mouth (see Luke 1:21-22). And Luke 1:23 reveals that when the days of his service at the temple were concluded, he silently returned to his home.

Just as the Lord had promised, Elizabeth became pregnant shortly thereafter. Verses 24 and 25 of Luke 1 tell us that she "hid herself for five months, saying, 'For in this way the Lord has dealt with me in days wherein He looked upon (me) to take away my reproach among men." Elizabeth conceived at a time when she should have worried more about iron-poor blood than birth control. God is always faithful. He does what He says He will do. We can count on it!

MARY RECEIVES A SPECIAL VISITOR—LUKE 1:26-38

Six months after Elizabeth became pregnant, another special visit was paid to one of her relatives. This kinswoman, a young lady named Mary, received an amazing message from the angel Gabriel. We read in Luke 1:26-27:

> Now in the sixth month, the angel Gabriel was sent from God to a city of Galilee, the name Nazareth,
> To a virgin engaged to a man whose name was Joseph of the house of David, and the name of the virgin, Mary.

The same angel who had confronted Zacharias in the temple journeyed to the town of Nazareth, in the region of Galilee. There, sent by God, he contacted Mary, an innocent, godly, young virgin who was engaged to a man named Joseph. Gabriel did not bring his amazing news to Joseph, for the carpenter would have no part in the events which were to take place. Zacharias had received the divine visit, because he would play an integral role in bringing John the Baptist into the world. The news brought to Mary by Gabriel concerned another sort of birth: a one-time-only virgin conception.

Said Gabriel to the young woman: "Hail! You who have been endued with grace, the Lord is with you" (Luke 1:28).

Like Zacharias, Mary became fearful. Scripture says that "she was greatly troubled at the saying and was considering of what sort a greeting this might be" (Luke 1:29). Heavenly visits weren't everyday occurrences, and Mary trembled in wonder and awe.

"Fear not," Gabriel reassured her, "for you have found grace with God" (1:30). Then he went on to tell her of the marvelous task for which she had been chosen:

> And behold you will conceive in your womb and you will bring forth a son and you will call His name Jesus.
>
> This one shall be great and He shall be called Son of (the) Most High and the Lord God shall give to Him the throne of His father David.
>
> And He shall reign over the house of Jacob forever and to His kingdom there shall be no end (Luke 1:31-33).

Elizabeth and Zacharias would name their miracle baby John, but Mary was instructed to call hers "Jesus." John would be "great" in the eyes of the Lord, but Jesus would be called the "Son of the Most High." In a day yet to come, He certainly will reign on the throne of David forever and ever. Hymnist John Newton certainly grasped that truth when he penned the lyrics to the last verse of his immortal "Amazing Grace! How Sweet the Sound":

> When we've been there ten thousand years,
> Bright shining as the sun,
> We've no less days to sing God's praise
> Than when we first begun.

BUT, HOW?

Upon hearing these remarkable words from God, Mary was instantly curious. "How shall this be since I am not knowing a man?" she asked Gabriel (Luke 1:34). Unlike Zacharias, Mary did not express unbelief; she did not request a sign; she did not doubt that the promised birth would take place. And so she was not punished for her honest inquisitiveness. She wanted to know *how* she would bear this son. She had never been with a man. She had never had a physical experience. How then, would she become pregnant with the holy child?

"The Holy Spirit shall come upon you," answered Gabriel, "and the power of the Most High shall overshadow you, wherefore also the one begotten shall be called holy, the Son of God" (Luke 1:35). The virgin conception of Christ would be wrought by a miracle, plain and simple. The power of God Himself through His Spirit would overwhelm the young virgin so that the God-man, Jesus, could enter the world through her womb.

Miracles happen. With perhaps a little object lesson in mind, Gabriel went on to explain to Mary that a supernatural conception had already occurred: her kinswoman Elizabeth had conceived a son in her old age. Once barren, the elderly lady was now in the sixth month of her pregnancy (Luke 1:36). She had not experienced the direct intervention of the Holy Spirit, as Mary would, but God had acted to render her aged womb fruitful.

The angel concluded his words to the virgin with this stirring statement, "For no word from God shall be impossible" (Luke 1:37). Isn't that tremendous? 1 Thessalonians 5:24 says, "Faithful is He who calls you, and He also will bring it to pass" (NASB). God always comes through—nothing is beyond the reach of His mighty hand.

Think a moment about Mary. She was engaged. What would people think when she became pregnant before the wedding? Her neighbors and relatives would fan the flames of gossip with innuendos about her premarital sex life. And what would Joseph do? Their wedding celebration, if in fact the marriage took place at all, would be marred by the sight of her protruding stomach—an unavoidable reminder of her condition.

Mary could have said to the angel, "I really appreciate your thinking of me, but why don't you get somebody else for this job?" That would have been the easy way out, and could well have been her response, but it wasn't. Instead, with simple trust and confidence in her God, she said merely this: "Behold the handmaid of the Lord. Be it unto me according to your word" (Luke 1:38). His mission accomplished, Gabriel departed. And sometime thereafter, the power of the Holy Spirit caused the virgin to conceive the Christ.

MARY VISITS ELIZABETH—LUKE 1:39-56

Let's face it—there weren't a whole lot of people to whom Mary could confide the news of Gabriel's visit. Her mother would have scolded her for having an over-active imagination, and then would have privately wondered if the prewedding pressure was getting to her dear little girl. Her sisters would have giggled about their sister on her "high horse". . . and then would have teased Mary for presuming to be blessed of God. Her aunts would have disapproved of her fanciful storytelling, and would have thankfully clucked to themselves that at least their daughters didn't need to fabricate tales to get attention. Her uncles would have seen Mary's account as an excuse for her indulgence in premarital lovemaking, an explanation for the pregnancy she suspected could happen. And she had always been such a good child!

There was one person though, who would understand: Elizabeth! And so Luke 1:39-40 reveals that Mary hurriedly packed her bags and journeyed south to the Judean city where Zacharias and Elizabeth lived. As she entered their home, Mary greeted Elizabeth.

We read in Luke 1:41 that "it came to be when Elizabeth heard the greeting of Mary, the baby leaped in her womb and Elizabeth was filled with the Holy Spirit." She explained this to Mary, lifting her voice to loudly cry, "Blessed are you among women, and blessed is the fruit of your womb. And whence is this to me that the mother of my Lord should come to me?" (1:42-43).

Talk about instant confirmation! Even within the womb, John the Baptist recognized the Savior and leaped in exultation. Even before his birth, John's delight was in the Lord . . . as it would be for the rest of his life. His devout mother could only exclaim in awe at the wondrous visit of Mary, the mother of the Lord!

This reminds me of a funny story about Christmas crowds. Some friends were standing in a long line at a mall cafeteria. In front of them was a lady who looked at least eight months pregnant and *tired*. Her husband and five-year-old son stood beside her—or rather, the husband stood; the little boy squirmed. Finally, bored with the monotony of standing in line, the kid cupped his hands to his mouth and, leaning against his mother's bulging stomach, shouted to the baby within, "Haallo in theere!" I don't guess that wiggly child would have been surprised to know that the unborn John the Baptist leaped in his mom's womb!

BLESSED IS SHE WHO HAS BELIEVED

With joy at the event, Elizabeth next exclaimed of her cousin Mary, "Blessed is she who believed, for it shall be completed, the things having been spoken to her by the Lord" (1:45). Mary was greatly honored among women. Unlike Zacharias, she had immediately trusted in the word of the angel of God.

"My soul is magnifying the Lord," cried Mary, "And my spirit rejoices in God my Savior" (1:46-47). What a beautiful statement! Does your soul magnify the Lord as you sit, studying His Word? Do you rejoice in Him? Is it an exciting experience to know Him? It was for Mary and Elizabeth. The picture presented in the Gospel of Luke is of two women on opposite ends of life's pole—one young, one old—eagerly discussing the amazing things which the Lord had permitted in their lives.

Notice that Mary says that she rejoices in God, her "Savior." She was not sinless, but had need of a Savior just as does every human being. She merely was rewarded with the distinct privilege of giving birth to Him.

Mary continued to speak in her worship of the Lord, saying, "He looked upon the low estate of His handmaid, for behold from now all generations shall call me blessed" (1:48). Women are too often reminded that it was a female who brought sin into the world when Eve snatched the first bite of apple in the garden of Eden. Let's not forget that a woman was also the instrument used by God to bring the Savior into the world, to remove the blight of sin. When Christ could have entered the world as the child of a prince, He chose to come through one of humble and low estate, a simple maiden.

"For the Mighty One did great things for me," said Mary, "and holy is His name" (1:49). As the writer of Psalm 48 exclaims, "Great is the Lord, and greatly to be praised" (48:1 NASB). And Psalm 71:19 echoes those sentiments with these words: "For Thy righteousness, O God, reaches to the heavens, Thou who hast done great things; O God, who is like Thee?" (NASB).

Mary continued her praise of the Lord, extolling that which He had done throughout the history of her people:

> And His mercy is from generation to generation to the ones fearing Him.
>
> He showed strength in His arm. He scattered the proud in the imagination of their hearts.
>
> He tore down princes from their thrones and exalted them of low estate.
>
> The hungry ones He filled with good and the rich ones He sent away empty.

And He helped Israel His servant that He might remember mercy.

Even as He spake to our fathers, to Abraham and his seed forever (Luke 1:50-55).

Mary's final reference to Abraham reminds us of the supernatural birth of Isaac. Mary was just a young lady, but she knew enough about Scripture to realize that if God could fill Sarah's barren womb, He could surely cause her to become pregnant while yet a virgin.

For three months Mary remained with Elizabeth, and then returned to her own home. You don't have to be a midwife to realize that Elizabeth's due date was fast approaching. She had reached the nine-month mark in her pregnancy, while Mary was some three months along in hers. It was time for the younger woman to go home, time to return to a place of security to await the birthday of her King, which would happen in just six short months.

THE BIRTH OF JOHN—LUKE 1:57-80

Just as the Lord said would happen, Elizabeth gave birth to a son. Great was the rejoicing of her friends, neighbors, and relatives, at this manifestation of God's mercy toward the aged woman.

Luke 1:59 reveals that on the eighth day after the child's birth, the neighbors and family came for the circumcision of the boy, in accordance with the law. They planned to name the baby after Zacharias. The proud father couldn't talk . . . but surely he'd want a Junior running around the house after so many years. Then came a huge surprise.

"No indeed," said Elizabeth, "but he shall be called John" (1:60).

The astounded onlookers argued with her, no doubt spouting comments like, "John? What do you mean, John? None of your relatives is named John!" They turned to the still-mute Zacharias, making signs, asking his opinion on the matter. Zacharias merely motioned for a writing tablet, upon which he indicated that John would indeed be the boy's name. At this, his tongue was loosened, and he began blessing God with all his might (see Luke 1:61-64). At his obedience, the Lord restored his voice, and Zacharias responded properly. The first words out of his mouth praised God!

How did the people react? Remember that when the supernatural touches the natural, fear is often the result. They were afraid . . . and reports of the matter soon filtered throughout the hill country of Judea. "What then shall this child be? For indeed the hand of the Lord is with him," they exclaimed (Luke 1:66).

Zacharias then began to prophesy. We realize that he must have understood what had happened to Mary—that the Savior dwelt in her womb—because he proclaimed:

> Blessed be the Lord God of Israel, for He has visited and made redemption for His people.
>
> And He has raised up a horn of salvation for us, in the house of David His servant—
>
> Even as He spoke by the mouth of His holy prophets from of old—
>
> Salvation from our enemies, and from the hand of all who are hating us;
>
> To show mercy toward our fathers, and to remember His holy covenant,
>
> The oath which He swore to Abraham our father,
>
> To give to us that we, being delivered from the hand of our enemies, might serve Him without fear,
>
> In holiness and righteousness before Him all our days (Luke 1:68-75).

And then, evidently holding the precious child John in his arms, Zacharias looked at his own much-loved son and uttered these prophetic statements:

And you, child, will be called the prophet of the Most
High; for you will go before the Lord to prepare His
ways;

To give to His people the knowledge of salvation, by
the forgiveness of their sins,

Because of the heart of mercy of our God, in that the
sun rising from on high shall visit us,

To shine upon those who sit in darkness and the
shadow of death, to guide our feet in the way of peace
(Luke 1:76-79).

An old gentleman, cradling a baby in his arms, knew that
the child would grow to be the forerunner of the Lord,
paving the way, preparing the hearts of men and women to
receive Him. And that is exactly what John did.

The Life of the Messenger

Thirty years later, while baptizing converts in the Jordan
River, John looked up to catch a glimpse of the sight he had
long awaited. Jesus the Messiah was approaching, walking
along the shore. "Behold, the Lamb of God who takes away
the sin of the world!" John exclaimed (John 1:29 NASB).
Sometime later, before his imprisonment and execution, John
explained his position to his own disciples, "Your yourselves
bear me witness, that I said, 'I am not the Christ,' but, 'I
have been sent before Him' " (John 3:28 NASB).

John the Baptist never claimed to be the Messiah. He
knew ever and always that his was a subordinate role: that of
the messenger or forerunner. It's important for us to realize
that the nature of his task did nothing to diminish the importance of that task. To God, all service for Him ranks the
same. The deeds performed by the retired fellow who sham-
poos the sanctuary carpet each month rank with the sermon-
izing of the most glib and godly evangelist. What is important is the spirit in which each chore is performed.

In Light of What We've Learned

In light of the fact that God appreciates the smallest deed done in His name as much as the most grandiose project undertaken to honor Him, why don't we rethink our gift-giving this Christmas? Instead of concerning ourselves with how large, how expensive, how impressive a present we purchase, perhaps we should strive to become more tuned in to the little things out there which can be performed to God's glory. Oh, we'll still splurge on our loved ones, yet let's not forget that often the most valuable of gifts costs very, very little . . . and may merely involve nothing more than some extra time.

For example, why not consider visiting a local nursing home with your children? Or prepare special Christmas cards for the shut-ins you know. Offer to babysit for a young mother whose two-year-old bundle of perpetual motion makes Christmas shopping a dreaded ordeal. Drive an older neighbor to her beauty appointment. Go caroling to the homes near your church. Send a card and an extra offering to a missionary. Make a special effort to visit any you know who are hospitalized; Christmas within white-washed institutional walls can be gloomy indeed.

I'll never forget the December evening when my friend Cliff was taken to the hospital for the last time. I live near the medical center, and when the phone call came informing me of my pal's condition, I was out the door and at the hospital before the ambulance arrived. Spying me from his stretcher as the attendants wheeled him past, Cliff whispered faintly, "We're close now."

Later that evening, when he was settled in his room, I had a chance to visit with him at greater length. "Is there anything you'd really like?" I asked him.

"I'd love some ice cream, just some ice cream," Cliff hoarsely replied.

"Nurse," I called, "my friend would like some ice cream. Could you get us some?"

"I'm sorry. Cafeteria's closed," she said.

I stepped out into the corridor. "Nurse, that man is dying. He wants some ice cream. Please!"

"Sorry, I can't do anything about it," came the reply.

She couldn't . . . but I could. I ran down the hall and hopped in the elevator. At ground level I took off, jogging down the road a few blocks to the ice cream shop. I don't even remember which one of the thirty-one flavors I ordered, but the kid behind the counter put it in a cup, and back to the hospital I ran. I watched Cliff eat his ice cream. We talked and we prayed together.

That was probably the nicest Christmas present I have ever been able to give. It cost less than two dollars and involved a little leg work. It brought a smile to the face of a dear, dying friend.

And I thought to myself that so many times we lavish folks with extravagant gifts at Christmas time. Our pride urges us to spend enormous amounts of money. We run up bills which will last till well past Easter. All that takes place, when maybe a little friendship, maybe a cup of ice cream, maybe a small dose of love, would be vastly more appreciated than all the costly items we scour the malls to buy.

OUR GIFT TO GOD

What makes the story of John the Baptist so special? It is his humility. It is each beautiful relationship which unfolds as Luke gives his account. It's Zacharias and Elizabeth. It's Mary and the Spirit of God. It's life going on and the beauty of things happening in God's will.

God wants *us* this Christmas. He wants to talk to us and hear from us. He wants to show us that the road we travel is not impossible, that His grace is sufficient, that His strength is made perfect in our weakness. The gift of ourselves is what we should wrap up and place under the tree for our Lord this season. That is what He truly desires.

Reflections for the season

1. God resists the proud, but gives grace to the humble.

2. With God, nothing is impossible!

3. The Lord makes everything beautiful in His time.

4. Reexamine your gift list this Christmas, and give more of yourself!

The Final Fulfillment
Luke 2:21-38

*K*ids and Christmas—although all of ours are over twenty now, they still act like youngsters when they come home for the holidays: piling into the den and spending the night before Christmas on the floor in sleeping bags. The excitement is electric!

It is such a joy to have little ones running around the house at Christmas, too. Up before dawn on the 25th to see if Santa has visited, preteen children rouse the adults as soon as the sun edges over the horizon. Even dear old Dad, who spent the night before assembling bicycles, is uncharitably tumbled out of the sack at dawn's early light. Santa has come! "Mom, Dad, Grandpa, look! Pretty packages!"

CHRISTMAS THROUGH KIDS' EYES

I have noticed over the years that children often get the funniest ideas about what's going on at Christmas. The sacred and secular images, to which we adults have grown accustomed, can evoke confused—and often comical—responses from youngsters. For example, one dad found himself calmly explaining to his three-year-old son on a December afternoon, "No Stevie, a reindeer is not a horse with a TV antenna on its head"!

And then there's the story I heard of the group of first graders who were told to draw pictures representing Christmas. Crayon renditions of Santa Claus, Christmas trees, wreaths, and candy canes were churned out. One little fellow drew a picture of a nativity scene. In his work of art, Mary and Joseph stood before the manger. Shepherds knelt nearby; animals milled about the stable. And off to one side, was a little fat man. "Who is he?" asked the teacher.

The response of the child was, "Oh, him? He's round John Burgeon!"

Isn't that great? I hope his mother pasted that piece of artwork in that kid's baby book. The same goes for another child's picture of the shepherds out in the field. These crayon shepherds weren't gazing at the star, or at the angelic host in the heavens, or even at their flocks. With the starlit evening sky as a backdrop, these shepherds were gathered round an old laundry tub. Said the six-year-old artist, "This is when the shepherds washed their socks by night." Another memento for posterity!

Then on the other hand, some kids nowadays are too sophisticated to even join in any of the north pole Christmas fantasy. You tell the Santa Claus story to a group of children, and you're likely to have some seven-year-old ask how many pounds of thrust the sleigh develops before it leaves the pad!

But kids do make Christmas special. They add a touch of wonder, a measure of mirth, a healthy dose of anticipation and excitement. And you know who else makes Christmas special? Grandparents, that's who.

OVER THE RIVER AND THROUGH THE WOODS

This past Christmas our own two small grandsons were home for the holidays. What a pleasure it was to watch little eyes, filled with sleep, suddenly twinkle with anticipation. "Look at all the presents! . . . Can I open 'em now?"

"Let's have breakfast first, and read the Christmas story, then you can."

And in the middle of breakfast, out pops the question, "Is it time now?"

"Not yet. Pretty soon." Of course, "pretty soon" seems like an eternity to wide-eyed, giggly, excited little ones.

Christmas truly is for kids. I'd forgotten how much fun and joy can come when children receive and give gifts. Ian, our oldest grandson, attacks packages with ferocious intensity, while Andrew, his one-year-old brother, is more the reserved, contemplative type. The contrast between the two made for high comedy last Christmas morn as we watched them operate. While Ian eagerly searched for still another present to rip into, Andrew lingered over his first package. Quickly Ian ran out of gifts and scampered to help Grandma and Grandpa open theirs. This done, he gave Andrew a hand, and it's a good thing. Andrew would probably still be under the tree if it weren't for the help of big brother!

In fact, Andrew became rather attached to our Christmas tree last year. The little rascal even tried to eat one of the shiny red glass balls hanging within reach. Thank goodness he didn't swallow any slivers, although he gave it a try. His parents carted him to the emergency room anyway, just to be sure. What a holiday!

Over the years, Pearl and I have received good training in the art of grandparenting. The two churches where I minister are located in lakeside recreational communities overflowing with retired folks. At Hide-A-Way Lake and Emerald Bay, we've seen firsthand how grandparents relate to their grandkids . . . and great-grandkids. We've witnessed grandparent survival tactics like planning the dear ones' stays during the week of vacation Bible school (you can stand just so much of a good thing, apparently). And of course any visit from the grandchildren calls for stocking up on hot dogs, potato chips, frozen pizzas, chocolate-chip cookies, and soda pop.

A gray-haired gent remarked after bidding his three grandsons goodbye, "I'm so tired after these seven days that when I bend over, I try to do several things while I'm down there!"

Yet, all kidding aside, there is nothing more beautiful than seeing three and sometimes four generations sitting together in our Christmas Eve services. From youngest to oldest, each lifts a lighted candle in the semidarkness, and sweetly sings the timeless words of "Silent Night." The glow from the candles is not all that warms the heart.

My point is that you just can't beat the influence of a godly older person on the life of a youngster. So if your children don't have grandparents of their own, adopt some! The benefits can be lifelong.

BITTER OR BETTER?

Another thing which I have noticed about the older folks from Hide-A-Way, Emerald Bay, and elsewhere, is that they tend to fall into one of two categories. They have either become *bitter* or *better* with age.

When we grow old, there emerges a conflict between being and doing. We are not able to perform as we once did. What we *are* becomes infinitely more important than what we are able to do. Some people react to their limitations with bitterness and resentment. But others respond to their old age, seeing it as a time of expanded horizons, not dead-end streets. These people, like rare wine, become better with age. They are a delight to the soul, examples worth imitating. We are going to meet two such terrific senior citizens, Simeon and Anna, as we consider a passage from the Gospel of Luke.

THE CHRISTMAS STORY

Luke, chapter 2, is one of the best-loved sections of all Scripture. The first twenty verses, especially, provide meat for sermons delivered from Christian pulpits across the world at yuletide. With warm fireplaces flickering in the background, fathers read the account to families gathered about glowing Christmas trees. Choirs joyously sing the words to beloved carols whose composers were inspired by the familiar story.

And it is beautiful to read of the humble birth of the Christchild—the King who is wrapped in swaddling cloths and laid in a rude trough in a crude stable, because there is no room in the inn (2:7). How well we can identify with the astonished shepherds who look up from their grazing flocks to find the still blackness of the night shattered by the angel of the Lord proclaiming the good news of the Savior's birth (2:11). The very heavens burst forth with a multitude of the angelic host praising God. In wonder, the shepherds trek into the town of Bethlehem. They kneel in adoration at the sight of the babe, and then return to their fields, glorifying the Lord with each step they take (2:13-20).

It is a truly marvelous story. . . but too often preachers, Sunday school teachers, moms and dads, go no farther. The remainder of Luke 2 is frequently neglected. We stop at the shepherds, and do not explore the sacred page to learn of the response to the birth of Messiah of two other godly people. And yet the account of Simeon and Anna is just as heartwarming as the story of the shepherds. It is every bit as moving, and just as indicative of God's incredible power. Let's look now at the text of Luke 2:21-38, and learn more of the earthly welcome accorded the King by two special senior citizens.

Born under the Law—Luke 2:21-24

Luke 2:21 states of the Christchild, "And when eight days were fulfilled to circumcise Him, and they called His name Jesus, which He was called by the angel before He was conceived in the womb." Galatians 4:4 tells that, "But when the fulness of the time came, God sent forth His Son, born of a woman, born under the Law" (NASB). Notice the phrase, "under the Law." This refers to the law given by God to the children of Israel through their leader, Moses. Christ was born "under," or subject to, this law. If He were to be able one day to function as our Redeemer, it was vital, a divine requirement, that He fulfill every section and subsection of that law. His life had to be absolutely perfect in every way. He could violate no portion of the God-ordained Jewish legal and moral code.

Before Jesus would even act for Himself, He was acted upon by parents who, as far as was humanly possible, observed these regulations. The first of the law's stipulations to be fulfilled happened when the child was named and circumcised eight days after His birth. For the Jewish male, circumcision is the mark of the Abrahamic Covenant; it is an ordinance explicitly instituted by God in Genesis 17, and prescribed in Leviticus 12:3. Jesus had to undergo that rite at eight days of age if He were to flawlessly live out the Mosaic Law. And so He did.

With His circumcision at the temple, came His naming. The babe was called Jesus, or "Savior," precisely as the angel had earlier instructed Mary (Luke 1:31). Mary and Joseph could take no chances with the precious treasure God had entrusted to them.

Jesus' parents continued to act in accordance with the law. Luke 2:22 tells us that "when the days of their purification were fulfilled according to the Law of Moses, they brought Him up to Jerusalem to present Him to the Lord." The time of this event was thirty-two days after Jesus' circumcision and naming. Forty days after His birth, Joseph and Mary packed up their infant son and journeyed the six miles from Bethlehem to the bustling city of Jerusalem.

People who live a distance from town know that you usually book a few appointments or plan on running several errands when you venture within the city limits. It's convenient; it saves time. As Mary and Joseph set out for Jerusalem with their month-and-a-half year old baby, they did so with two errands in mind as well.

First, Jewish law stated that a woman was religiously unclean for forty days following the birth of a son. Once that time passed, it was necessary to undergo a rite of purification, in keeping with the law. Only through that ceremony could a Jewish woman be made right religiously again.

Additionally, it was necessary for Mary and Joseph to present their baby boy in the temple in Jerusalem, because He was their firstborn. In Exodus 13:2, we read this command of the Lord given to Moses, "Sanctify to Me every firstborn, the first offspring of every womb among the sons of Israel, both of man and beast; it belongs to Me" (NASB). It was the law that every firstborn male be dedicated to the Lord for service in His temple (see also Luke 2:23). This was true of each Israelite tribe, except the Levites. Every son born into the tribe of Levi was automatically destined to be a priest when he grew up.

Jesus was not born into the tribe of Levi, but into that of Judah. Because of this, the law stipulated an action which could be taken to free Him from this priestly obligation. When His parents publicly consecrated their child to the Lord at the temple, a redemption tax of five shekels of silver could also be paid so that the child would be freed from priestly service later in life (see Numbers 18:16; Unger 1966, 915). Mary and Joseph journeyed to Jerusalem with the intention of paying that tax.

By today's standards, a shekel of silver would be worth about sixty-four cents. Five shekels, then, would have been worth around three dollars and twenty cents. That doesn't sound like much, until you consider that the average daily wage in the time of Christ was only about sixteen or eighteen cents. It would therefore require the wages of seventeen to twenty days to pay the temple tax. That was quite a bit of money, and Mary and Joseph weren't exactly wealthy.

They were, on the contrary, very, very poor. Think about it. The trip to Bethlehem from Nazareth was lengthy, and must have been costly. For the last forty days, the little family, knowing of their coming mission to Jerusalem, had had to hole up in the small city of Jesus' birth, rather than make the long journey home to Nazareth. They'd probably been able to find accommodations at a local inn, once many of the tourists had vacated. It's possible that Joseph had been able to hire himself out as a carpenter on some construction projects in Bethlehem during that month, to help make ends meet. Still, it's certain that with hotel bills and nonresident expenses, times were tough financially for the young couple.

We know that there wasn't much extra cash because of what is stated in Luke 2:24, where we read that Mary and Joseph came to Jerusalem "to offer a sacrifice according to what has been said in the Law of the Lord, 'A pair of turtle-doves, or two young pigeons.'" This sacrifice was an essential part of the purification rite spoken of earlier. In Leviticus 12:6-8, the law calls for the mother of a newborn to bring a one-year-old lamb to the priest at the temple for a burnt offering. The woman also had to bring a young pigeon or turtledove as a sin offering. Such animals, especially the lamb, did not come cheaply, yet a blood sacrifice was necessary if the woman was to become religiously pure again.

What if a couple simply could not afford to purchase a yearling lamb? Then, as the passage in Leviticus goes on to reveal, two turtledoves or two young pigeons could be substituted for the lamb. This was only allowed when couples were poor—a wealthy man and woman could not skimp on the sacrifice merely to save money. Mary and Joseph were among the poverty-stricken who could not afford to purchase a lamb for sacrifice, and instead bought two pigeons or turtledoves for one-tenth the price. Into what humble circumstances was our Lord born! Realizing that surely makes the passage in 2 Corinthians 8:9 come alive, doesn't it? There we read of Christ, "Though He was rich, yet for your sake

He became poor, that you through His poverty might become rich" (NASB).

Mary and Joseph did make the journey to Jerusalem. As the curtain opens on our scene there, we meet a beautiful old man. The Scripture tells us that "there was a man in Jerusalem whose name was Simeon; and this man was righteous and devout, looking for the consolation of Israel; and the Holy Spirit was upon him" (Luke 2:25). Immediately, we know four things about this elderly gentleman.

First, Simeon was "righteous." He desired to see goodness and holiness enacted in his life. Such people are given a wonderful promise in Matthew 5:6, where Christ says, "Blessed are those who hunger and thirst for righteousness, for they shall be satisfied" (NASB). And Simeon was satisfied when he, at long last, was given a glimpse of the Savior.

We also know that Simeon was "devout." The word *devout,* in this usage, indicates an anxiety to do well. It means "to take hold of with reverence." It is an attitude of the heart. Man looks on the outward appearance and judges another as righteous by his actions; only God can look upon the heart and know if one is truly devout, as was Simeon.

This old man also constantly looked for something: "the consolation of Israel." When things get bad for us, we often say, "Well, at least we have one consolation. . . ." Israel, in Simeon's day, was under Roman domination. The single consolation to which the nation could cling was the promise of God that the Messiah would come. He was their last hope, and Simeon probably spent many a night on his knees praying for the arrival of this King. He fully and eagerly anticipated the coming of the Holy One.

One more thing which we read of Simeon was that "the Holy Spirit was upon him." The Bible never minces words. The Holy Spirit was not *in* Simeon because the Spirit had not yet come to indwell believers. It would be thirty-three years later when Christ, in the upper room, would promise His disciples that God's Spirit would live within them (see John 14:17). Simeon simply experienced the Holy Spirit's presence upon him so that he might perform special functions of service. He was a man who walked with God, and God used him, and so the Holy Spirit was with him temporarily.

Simeon was a classic example of a man who had not become bitter with age, but better. Some of us do not grow old so sweetly. We find old age the height of frustration. Why? It's because we cannot perform as we once did. The old body just isn't what it used to be. We tire more easily; the ticker skips a beat or two occasionally; the eyes don't allow us to read everything we desire. And so we indulge in self-pity, becoming cranky, cantankerous, critical, and just plain tough to live with.

Psychiatrist and theologian Paul Tournier writes of growing old in his *Seasons of Life:*

> The die is cast. That which I have been able to do, to learn, or to acquire is gradually losing its value. The *doing* and the *having* are giving way to the *being.* What is important for the aged is not what they are still able to do, nor yet what they have accumulated and cannot take with them. It is what they are (Tournier 1963, 54-55).

The era for Geritol and pacemakers is also the time when, as Tournier suggests, what we are becomes far more important than what we are able to do. God designs our bodies to slow down in old age, so that He can refine the being, rather than the doing, in our lives. Recognizing and accepting that truth is the beginning of becoming better with age. Indeed, Simeon had learned the priceless lesson that what a man is vastly outweighs what a man does in the eternal scheme of things. And thus, with the Holy Spirit upon him, he was righteous, devout, ever and always looking for the consolation of Israel.

What is more, God had made him a marvelous promise. Luke 2:26 says of Simeon, "And it had been revealed to him by the Holy Spirit that he would not see death before he had seen the Lord's Christ." Through faith, Simeon knew for a fact that before he died, he would gaze upon the face of the Messiah, the consolation of Israel.

Reading of Simeon's intimacy with the Lord reminds me of a portion of the story of Abraham. Just after God had revealed to Abraham that his wife would have a child within a year, the Lord asked this question: "Shall I hide from Abraham what I am about to do?" (Genesis 18:17 NASB). The answer was no; the Lord went on to disclose His plans for the judgment of Sodom and Gomorrah. As Psalm 25:14 puts it, "The secret of the LORD is for those who fear Him, And He will make them know His covenant" (NASB).

Like Simeon, the more we get to know the Lord, the more we're going to love Him, and the more He's going to share with us the secrets of His heart. Part of spiritual growth involves the sheer joy of having the Lord impart truth to us in the times we spend with Him in prayer and in the reading of His Word. It is a delight to partake of precious, secret, special thoughts offered us as we grow closer to Him. As Proverbs 3:32 states, "For the crooked man is an abomination to the LORD; But He is intimate with the upright" (NASB; see also Amos 3:7, Daniel 2:19).

LED BY THE LORD TO A LONG-AWAITED REWARD

No wonder Simeon received God's seal of approval! He was an upright man, always open and vulnerable to the leading of the Lord. We read in Luke 2:27 that Simeon "came in the Spirit into the temple . . . when the parents brought in the child Jesus that they might do for Him according to the custom of the Law." The Spirit of God directed the elderly man to the temple on the specific day and at the specific hour when Mary and Joseph arrived to present the Christchild. Perhaps Simeon hadn't even considered walking to the temple at that time. Then came a message from the Lord and he got moving as fast as his arthritic legs would carry him. God's timing is always perfect, and His prompting is never to be ignored.

A man, who like Simeon is truly walking with the Lord, will be open to His direction. Proverbs 3:5-6 describes the pattern well:

> Trust in the LORD with all your heart,
> And do not lean on your own understanding.
> In all your ways acknowledge Him,
> And He will make your paths straight (NASB).

And Psalm 37:23-24 is a lesson in readiness and trust:

> The steps of a good man are ordered by the LORD; and he delighteth in his way. Though he fall, he shall not be utterly cast down; for the LORD upholdeth him with his hand (KJV).

First, Simeon had a *revelation* from the Lord that he would not taste death before beholding the Christ. Second, he was given a *direction,* a burden, a concern to come into the temple at a certain hour. There he saw the child Jesus, the Savior, whose coming he had long awaited in patient expectation. How did he react?

Luke 2:28 tells us that Simeon took the Christchild into his arms, and cradling him there, he "blessed God" (Luke 2:28). Babies are hard to resist, especially at six weeks of age, when the newborn redness and wrinkles have begun to be replaced by layers of chubbiness. Such gurgling and cooing infants seem to beg to be held, and Simeon was by no means immune to the appeal of Mary and Joseph's little one.

Yet he realized that this was no ordinary baby, for he began blessing God.

How does one bless God? The P.A.T. formula comes to mind. We bless God through our P.A.T.: praise, adoration, and thanksgiving. I imagine that bursting from Simeon's lips was something very much like the doxology which we sing on Sundays:

> Praise God from whom all blessings flow,
> Praise Him all creatures here below,
> Praise Him above, ye heav'nly host,
> Praise Father, Son and Holy Ghost.

DEPARTING IN PEACE

After Simeon blessed God, he said:

> Now Lord, let Your bond-servant be departing in peace according to Your word;
> For my eyes have seen Your salvation,
> Which You prepared in the presence of all peoples,
> A light for revelation to the Gentiles and
> the glory of Your people Israel (Luke 2:29-32).

Once he had seen the Christchild, Simeon was ready for his own coming demise. He was prepared to go home to be with the Lord. The word *depart* is basically the same one, with a different prefix, which the apostle Paul uses in Philippians 1:23, where he writes, "But I am hard-pressed from both directions, having the desire to depart and be with Christ, for that is very much better" (NASB). The word means to pull up the tent stakes, to turn loose of the ropes so that one might set sail. It conveys the idea of leaving behind the temporary in order to gain the permanent. In Simeon's case, he was essentially saying, "I am ready to depart, Lord. My life has been fulfilled. I have glimpsed that which You have promised, and it is enough. I am ready to go."

In a nutshell, Simeon's response should be a description of the death of every believer. I think once again of my friend Cliff. One day, close to the end, as I stood before his bedside, he whispered the words, "No trouble. No trouble." Days later he was practically incoherent, teetering on the brink of death. The night before had been a fitful one for Cliff, according to the nurse, and so I stood beside his bed for a few moments, and then I said, "Thou wilt keep him in perfect peace whose mind is stayed on thee" (Isaiah 26:3 KJV). Cliff just started repeating the words in a low murmur, "Peace, perfect peace, peace, perfect peace." He was ready to depart, to pull up the tent stakes, to cross from the night of mortal sickness into the light of eternity. Two days later, I preached his triumphant funeral service on a cold, blustery Christmas Eve afternoon.

Cliff's funeral was triumphant because he knew Jesus Christ as his personal Savior. He experienced firsthand the salvation of the Lord. So did Simeon. As the elderly man proclaimed while holding the baby in his arms, "For my eyes have seen Your salvation" (Luke 2:30).

As we grow older, some of us begin to feel awkward in our relationships with the Lord. We can't mow the church lawn or help build the playground equipment or stay awake during board meetings or even make it to every service, especially the evening ones. But salvation is not found in a performance! It is, as Simeon discovered, found in a Person. Who would have thought that in the next thirty-three years, the child cradled in Simeon's arms would heal blind eyes, would calm a stormy sea, would feed the multitudes, and would ultimately die upon Calvary's cross for man's sin? Salvation is wrapped up in that tiny child who became that sinless man. It involves a relationship with Him, not human works and not human performance.

Besides that, it is a salvation open to all who will believe!

As Simeon, still holding the baby Jesus, goes on to say of God's salvation, it is that "which You prepared in the presence of all peoples" (Luke 2:31). Salvation is not earmarked for a select group, but rather, as Colossians 3:11 states, it is "a renewal in which there is no distinction between Greek and Jew, circumcised and uncircumcised, barbarian, Scythian, slave and freeman, but Christ is all, and in all" (NASB)

Salvation also involves, according to Simeon, "A light of revelation to the Gentiles and the glory of Your people Israel" (Luke 2:32). And Christ is both the light and the glory of His people. Jesus Himself said that He was the light of the world (John 8:12). Cries the psalmist, "Lift up your heads, O you gates; lift them up, you ancient doors, that the King of glory may come in. Who is this King of glory? The LORD Almighty—he is the King of glory" (Psalm 24:9-10 NIV). He brings revelation to the Gentiles and glory to the house of Israel—to all, that is, who receive Him. This, Simeon understood.

TURNING TO MOM AND DAD

Yet Scripture reveals that Mary and Joseph were surprised at the old man's remarks. Jesus' "father and mother were marveling at the things which were being said about Him," says Luke 2:33. Here was this distinguished old gentleman—exuding the fragrance of a righteous life, displaying the characteristics of a devout man of God, controlled by the Holy Spirit—uttering such incredible words about their boy!

The parents must have said something to draw Simeon's attention away from the child momentarily, for we read in Luke 2:34-35 that he turned to the couple, and . . .

> . . . blessed them, and said to Mary . . . 'Behold, this child is set for the falling and rising of many in Israel, and for a sign to be spoken against—And a sword shall

pass through your soul—in order that the thoughts of many hearts might be revealed.'

Simeon first blessed Mary and Joseph. Why? I think he blessed Mary because she was willing to be the vehicle through whom the child was born. I think he blessed Joseph because Joseph was willing to take her into his home and care for her, even though she was pregnant with the child of the Holy Spirit. The pair received blessings because they were willing to cooperate with the divine program. And with this blessing came three prophetic statements about Christ.

CHOOSING SIDES

First, according to Simeon, Jesus was to be "set for the falling and rising of many in Israel." Some will fall, and some will rise when they meet Christ. The reason is given in 1 John 5:12: "He who has the Son has the life; he who does not have the Son of God does not have the life" (NASB). Jesus Christ was destined to literally split humanity into two groups: those who believe on Him, and those who do not. It happened even as He hung upon the cross. Two thieves were crucified alongside Him. Only one called out, "Jesus, remember me when You come into Your kingdom!" And only that one was told these words, "Truly I say to you, today you shall be with Me in Paradise" (Luke 23:42-43 NASB). Falling and rising—those are the results, depending on our responses to Him.

Simeon goes on to tell Mary and Joseph that their child was destined to be "a sign to be spoken against." In Luke 4:28-29, we read of the rage which engulfed those in a synagogue listening to Jesus. They cast Him out of the city and fully intended to throw Him off a cliff. Later He would be unjustly tried and sentenced. "Crucify Him!" shouted the angry mob; Pilate released a murderer named Barabbas and sent an innocent man to die on a hill outside Jerusalem (see Mark 15:14-15). Truly He was "spoken against."

And Simeon further promises Mary that a "sword" shall pass through her soul. Years later, tears would pour from her eyes as she watched her beloved Son die in agony at Calvary. For a mother, there is no sharper sword imaginable than the death of a child. Jesus' suffering severed Mary's heart in two.

With amazing accuracy, Simeon predicted future events in the life of the child he held in his arms. He also revealed the purpose of each episode of trial, and that was: "In order that the thoughts of many hearts might be revealed" (Luke 2:35). Calvary did that. It was a time of choosing sides, and the choice remains ours today.

Will we be numbered among those who mocked Christ on the cross? Will we ignore His offer of salvation? Or will we find ourselves like those who wept bitterly at His suffering? Will we mourn the fact that our sins virtually nailed Him to the cross, and will we call upon Him as Savior and Lord? The choice is ours. And every single time the gospel of Jesus Christ is presented, the thoughts of the hearts of people are revealed, just as Simeon, nearly two thousand years ago, said they would be. The time for acceptance or rejection of Christ is today. In the words of 2 Corinthians 6:2, "Now is the accepted time; behold, now is the day of salvation" (KJV).

INTRODUCING ANNA—LUKE 2:36-38

Just as Simeon finished uttering his prophecies, another figure came onto the scene, a woman who had perhaps overheard all that had been said. Luke 2:36-37 tells us:

> And there was a prophetess, Anna, the daughter of Phanuel, of the tribe of Asher. She was advanced in her days greatly, having lived with a husband seven years from her virginity. And then as a widow to the age of

eighty-four and she departed not from the temple, serving night and day with fastings and prayers.

It's wise not to call a woman old—mature, maybe, but not old. The Greek text avoids doing that in the case of Anna, whose name means "grace" or "favor." Instead of being old, we read that Anna was "advanced in her days greatly." Isn't that a tactful way of putting it? The plain truth is that Anna was eighty-four years young. Can a woman be beautiful in her advanced period of life? Oh, yes, as we shall see from the example of this special lady.

Though in her eighties, Anna wasn't retired. She was a prophetess—an individual who, before the divine revelation of the Lord was complete, would receive knowledge from God and disclose it, and who also would expound upon the divine revelation which had already been given—explaining it, clarifying it. Apparently, much of Anna's ministry involved prayer and fasting in the Lord's temple. In fact, she never left the place!

Why was she free to remain at the temple twenty-four hours a day? It's simple. She was a widow. Seven years after her marriage, her husband had died, leaving Anna with some choices. She could have returned to her family and waited for another husband. Or she could have retreated from life, going home to grow more bitter with each passing year. She might well have spent the rest of her life in anger and resentment at the premature loss of her beloved man. Yet she did neither of these.

Therapy for a Broken Heart

Corrie ten Boom once said, "When you find time on your hands, get on your knees." And this is what Anna chose to do. She decided that the house of the Lord was the place for her, and she dedicated the remainder of her years—perhaps as many as sixty or more—to serving Him. Sorrow might have made her rebellious and resentful, but it didn't. Instead, sorrow transformed Anna into a beautiful example of kindness, softness, and sensitivity. She knew that the Father's hand never causes His child a needless tear, and so she made the most of her widowhood. She was not lonely but loving— a woman who refused to be destroyed by a broken heart.

A lady told me one time, "When my husband died, my life stopped."

"Did it?" I asked. "Don't you know that the Lord still has things for you to do?" She stared blankly at me in return, and then we discussed the example of Anna.

Anna fled to God. When a woman dares to leave the past alone and refuses to be dependent upon memories for happiness, she opens the door for God to do a tremendous work in her life. As she faces the present, a supernatural peace is able to flood her heart. As Anna discovered, immersing oneself in activity for the glory of God is marvelous therapy for a broken heart. Even though she was advanced in years, she was still serving Him. And she was rewarded with the privilege of viewing the Messiah.

Scripture reveals that as Simeon continued to hold Jesus, Anna approached. She wanted to know what he was so excited about. Do you think that Anna knew Simeon? I do. I figure that they were both at the temple quite a bit. I imagine that Anna saw in Simeon a distinguished older gentlemen whom she admired, and that he viewed her as a godly woman who had triumphed over impossible circumstances in her life, and who was living for the glory of God. Naturally, Anna wanted to know what brought forth the joy in Simeon's voice, and so she came bursting onto the scene. Immediately, with her prophetic insight, she knew.

Luke 2:38 tells us that Anna "began giving thanks to God, and continued speaking of Him to all those who were looking for the redemption of Jerusalem." At the crowning moment of her life, Anna did two things. She praised God with great thanksgiving. And she told everyone she knew of the good news of the Messiah. Whereas Simeon had looked for the "consolation of Israel," Anna addressed those who were "looking for the redemption of Jerusalem." Not only did she see Jerusalem as being in bondage to Rome, but also enslaved to sin and death. And here was the Christ, come to set His people free.

What wondrous news! Anna couldn't keep it to herself, either. Like the woman in John 4:28-29, who encountered Jesus at the well and marveled at His knowledge of her, Anna's tongue was loosened so that all might know that she had seen the redemption of Jerusalem. It was much too good to keep to herself!

Parting Shots

One of my seventyish pals told me one time, "I am not suffering from old age. I just have youth deficiency!" Whatever name you give them, the upper decades of life offer us the opportunity to grow bitter or better.

We can become like the distinguished elderly gentleman Simeon, reverent in our walk with God, having learned to give up on performance as such and become be-ers rather than do-ers.

Even if our path has been strewn with stumbling blocks, hurts, and broken dreams, as was Anna's, we can continue to draw nearer and nearer to the Lord, as she did. Diligent prayer and study of His Word are two means by which we can serve the Lord in gladness, no matter what our physical limitations. Anna, in her later life, apparently spent much of her time in prayer. Can we not do the same? As we look for His return, we'll find our broken hearts healed by the tremendous therapy of pressing toward the mark, where we will hear, "Well done, thou good and faithful servant!"

The beautiful thing to remember is that we can start today, this Christmas season, without delay. As one of our cooks at camp used to say, "Sittin' ain't gonna get it done!" Time's a wasting! Bitter . . . or better? The choice is yours.

Reflections for the season

1. Are you becoming bitter or better at this stage of development?

2. As you are getting older, are you concentrating on the *being,* rather than the *doing* in your life?

3. Learning to be a servant is a required course in the divine curriculum designed for us.

4. It is never too late to let God change you.

The Form of a Servant
Philippians 2:1-11

*F*inding the right Christmas present for some people is rough. I ought to know. Although my wife believes that a woman's place is in the mall, and that when the going gets tough, a woman goes shopping, I have been the one to do most of the Christmas shopping in our family through the years. At least I've been in charge of purchasing the gifts for our five children . . . and that's nothing to sneeze at.

While I'm ambling through the malls each December, I make a practice of studying the other shoppers. I people-watch. Preachers do that, you know—it's called gathering material for illustrations. By the way, you can do this at airports, too—it works just as well. Either place, you're guaranteed to see some strange sights. I am often rewarded with one gem or another. It's interesting, but the season of good will toward men seems to have very little effect on the species *homo sapiens shoppus*—that breed of human who frequents the shopping centers.

The last time I set out to Christmas shop, I decided to make a conscious effort to notice how many times people stood up for their "rights," and how many times they yielded their prerogatives for the sake of others. I watched department store entrances to see who held the door for whom, and who stepped aside to let others pass. I scrutinized crowds at cash registers to see who fought to keep his or her place in line, and who jockeyed for position. I kept an eye peeled in the parking lots to see who zipped into a space in front of whom, and also to observe the reaction of the "zippee" to the "zipper." It was an education! I found that most of us are extremely concerned with protecting our "rights"—including our places in line and the parking spaces we've staked out. We don't naturally surrender what we feel is due us. On the other hand, we're always ready for a free ride when the opportunity presents itself. We are, in other words, a "me-first" generation. No matter what we profess and confess, we seem terribly impressed with ourselves and with our rights.

WHY THE FREE RIDES?

"Me-firstness" seeps into all facets of life. An example of this which really hit home took place in one of my favorite bookstores. I often drop in to check out the new volumes at this shop, which is located a few blocks from Dallas Seminary. One day while I was browsing, a young man strode to the counter and plopped down a stack of books. "I'm a student at the seminary," he told the clerk. "I guess you have a discount for me." That remark, coupled with the young man's attitude, struck a sore spot with me.

I almost said to the kid, "I buy ten times the number of volumes you do in this bookstore and I have never once asked for a discount, nor do I intend to. The people who own this place are Christians, and they have needs, too!" But I restrained myself in righteous indignation, figuring the kid just had a lot to learn and, anyway, I didn't know him well enough to become his teacher. To be honest, I hope he's reading this.

We don't deserve the special privileges which me-firstness

seeks. Clergymen, be warned: what follows may ruffle your feathers. Yet what really riles me more than anything is the attitude among some men of the cloth that everyone else is supposed to minister to them. We preachers have got people so well trained that a minister can't buy his own lunch or pay for his own green fees—someone else does it for him. The privileged-status syndrome must start early, because even a wet-eared seminarian feels he deserves a special discount! I tell my congregations, how about letting the pastor (if he can afford it) pay your way once in a while, just like everybody else? Occasionally, let him materially minister to you. We're not talking about big expenditures, but a few of the niceties: lunches, parking charges, tips, or frozen yogurt all around.

You see, none of us really has any rights in this world—not shoppers, not ministers, no one. We don't have the right to be treated with special privileges. The only privilege any of us as Christians really possesses is the right to be servants.

Servants aren't concerned with haggling for discounts, snatching parking spaces, palming off green fees, and generally using others for selfish gratification. Servants are concerned with serving—with meeting the needs of other people. Servants of Jesus are dedicated to opening doors to the hearts of people so that the reality of Christ's message might spill forth into the life of another. And, make no mistake about it, we are called to be servants for Jesus' sake.

THE ULTIMATE SERVANT

You see, Jesus was a servant—the ultimate servant.

As His birth was, by our standards, an event encased in humility, so was His life upon earth. He lived and died with the interests of others at heart—the interests of many, in fact, who hated Him. He tabernacled or "tented" among us for thirty-three years, and during that time He did nothing that was self-serving or self-seeking. Sacrifice was the rule, not the exception . . . and though it involved unimaginable personal sacrifice at Calvary, Jesus sought only to do the will of the Father (see Matthew 26:39).

Certainly these qualities are evident as one reads of Jesus' life in the Gospels. Yet Christ's humility also shines forth in the writings of the apostles and other Christians who produced the rest of the New Testament. As we consider a passage from the book of Philippians, we'll see how vividly and clearly the apostle Paul presents the Savior as a servant. And His service for our sakes lies at the very heart of Christmas.

THE BOOK OF PHILIPPIANS

The Epistle to the Philippians seems an unlikely place to base a chapter on Christmas. Usually Christmas messages center on Luke 2 or Matthew 2, or perhaps on some of the prophecies surrounding Christ's birth. The more mature believers might tackle John 1. But Philippians? That's not about Christmas! Or so some might say. I disagree . . . and I hope that the comments which follow will be meaningful and helpful to you this season.

The apostle Paul finds himself in a Roman jail at the time he writes the letter to the Christians at Philippi. Epaphroditus, who has brought a gift from the church, will be returning to Philippi soon, so Paul seizes the opportunity to correspond with his beloved flock there (4:18). He is extremely close to the Philippian believers. In the beginning of the letter, he writes that he longs for them with all the affection of Christ Jesus, and he expresses his prayer that their love might abound all the more (1:8-9).

The first chapter of the epistle also contains a sort of missionary report, because the church forms part of the backbone of financial support for Paul's ministry. We know this because, in Philippians 4, Paul mentions that the Christians at Philippi have sent a fragrant offering of sacrifice to meet his needs while imprisoned (4:18). He is exceedingly grateful for their contribution. Because of their loving concern and material support, Paul makes sure that his friends know that the spread of the gospel has not stopped, although he has been under lock and key, probably under house arrest. The hubbub surrounding his imprisonment has actually worked to propagate the good news of Christ, sparking curiosity on the part of the Praetorian guard and emboldening other Christians in Rome to speak out for the Savior (1:12-18).

All that news is very positive, yet Philippians is more than a missionary report; it is a love letter. Paul cares deeply for his friends at Philippi, and at the same time, he fully realizes that his life is hanging in the balance. At any hour an order could come for his execution. Welling up within the apostle, then, is the emotion of the fact that this could be it, that God could very well call him home today, tomorrow, a week from now. So he assures his loved ones with these words, "For to me, to live is Christ, and to die is gain" (1:21 NASB). He is not afraid to die, yet he goes on to express the heart-wrenching conflict he feels within: "But I am hard-pressed from both directions, having the desire to depart and be with Christ, for that is very much better; yet to remain on in the flesh is more necessary for your sake" (1:23-24 NASB).

Why does Paul feel he must continue to live for the sake of his dear ones at Philippi? It's because there are some problems within the church. With a lump in his throat, the apostle plunges into chapter 2, where he seeks to deal with some of these difficulties confronting the Philippian flock. Each waking hour may be Paul's last; it's now or never if he is to exhort his friends to get their acts together on some crucial issues.

A CHURCH IN CONFLICT

The trouble at Philippi centers around two women named Euodoia and Syntyche, who are embroiled in controversy.

Their battles are dividing the congregation, so much so that Paul urges them to "live in harmony in the Lord" (4:2). The fussing and feuding of these two ladies are affecting the testimony of the entire church. It is a potentially devastating situation. As Paul well knows, unchecked conflict within a congregation can have fatal repercussions in the life of a church body.

An abandoned Protestant church located in a section of northern Berlin stands as a graphic example of the dangers of conflict. The building of the Church of the Reconciliation, as it is called, is found in East Berlin. Yet its front sidewalk is in the West, and the ten-feet-tall Berlin Wall effectively assures that never the twain shall meet (Tan 1984, 542).

A church struggling against itself can be very much like that Church of the Reconciliation—useless in the cold reality of life. Strife within a body of believers can symbolically seal the door of a sanctuary as effectively as any Berlin Wall, keeping outsiders from seeking comfort inside, because there is none to be found. The people have ceased to be servants; instead, the members are caught up in the conflict. The unsaved world is forgotten, as are the pressing personal needs of those within. There comes an exodus of neutral parties and all who are left are the side-takers. It is pitiful, and I've seen it happen too many times, even in conservative, evangelical churches. Afterward, the only time the sanctuary is filled is when the Christmas and Easter crowds make their semiannual Sunday morning pilgrimages.

WHY DO WE COME TO CHURCH?

Paul desperately desires that the Philippians avoid such spiritual deadness. So he encourages them with the opening words of Philippians 2:

> If there is therefore any encouragement in Christ, if there is any persuasion of love, if there is any fellow-

ship of the Spirit, if there are any tenderheartednesses and compassions, make full my joy, in order that you may be of the same mind, having the same love, of one mind, thinking the one thing, doing nothing according to self-seeking, nor according to empty glorying, but in lowliness of mind considering one another as excelling yourselves; not considering each his own things, but also each one the things of others. Let this mind be in you which was also in Christ Jesus (Philippians 2:1-5).

As we read those words, let us remember that Paul is languishing under Roman arrest. He is not free to travel to his Bible classes and churches; his contact with other Christians is limited. Perhaps he strongly feels the need himself for the "encouragement in Christ," "the persuasion of love," "the fellowship of the Spirit," and the "tenderheartednesses and compassions" of which he speaks. Certainly he desires that the believers at Philippi would be of the same mind in manifesting these qualities among themselves. If that were to happen, says the apostle, his joy would then be made "full."

Encouragement may involve a pat on the back, an honest recognition of talent or skill, a friendly word spoken at an opportune time. Love is simply that—the genuine, willful expression of human affection. The fellowship of the Spirit is the wonderful bond of unity which the Spirit of God enables Christians to experience because He indwells each one. Tenderheartednesses and compassions are acts of love and kindness. They involve the tangible meeting of needs, the willingness to become constructively involved in the lives of others. Combined, these qualities explain the reasons we band together in a church body, and, if missing from a congregation, their loss can strike a death blow to the life of a church.

Think about it a moment. Why do you come to church anyway? Many of us come mainly to hear a message to inspire us. Especially at Christmas time, we come in anticipation of receiving a blessing that will set the stage for our own celebration. We come so we can be "fed." This may anger some people, but folks, these should *not* be the reasons why we come to church!

Just as the apostle Paul exhorts his flock at Philippi, we Christian church-goers should be in the business of encouraging, loving, providing fellowship, and demonstrating tenderheartedness and compassion. We should not be as concerned with having our own needs met in these areas, as with meeting the needs of others along these lines. We should be servants, one to another.

God brings us to church on Sunday so that we might offer a word of encouragement to someone sitting in the congregation who is about ready to throw in the towel, to give up on life. Maybe it's family trauma, a battle with an extended illness, or job difficulties—whatever it is that has forced that man or woman down into the dumps, it is our job to be an encourager.

It's our task to show love as well. How long has it been since you have told somebody in your church, other than a family member, that you care about him or her? Quite a while, you say? And yet there are men, women, and children sitting out there who desperately need to know that somebody is concerned. Spoken words of affirmation and affection are essential!

And fellowship—how many months has it been since you invited someone from your midst home for Sunday dinner? The Christian world and its churches are filled with lonely, hurting people who shouldn't have to be lonely because of the unity of the body of Christ. Like the desperate multitudes upon whom Jesus felt compassion because they wandered like "sheep without a shepherd" (Matthew 9:36), our sanctuaries are brimming with the lost, the forlorn, the forsaken, and the hopeless.

Finally, when is the last time you reached out to another in genuine compassion? Have you dropped an extra check in the collection plate for a struggling family lately? Have you offered to babysit the child of a young mother whose own mother is having surgery Monday morning? Have you driven an elderly woman to a doctor's appointment? Have you asked anyone who has a need how you might help? Jesus Himself assured His disciples, "For whoever gives you a cup of water to drink because of your name as followers of Christ, truly I say to you, he shall not lose his reward" (Mark 9:41 NASB). We have got to be in the business of meeting the needs of our brothers and sisters in Christ!

You see, the desires for encouragement, love, fellowship, and compassion are common to us all. I truly believe that each individual Christian will be graded on how he or she responds to these needs. In the life of a church and in eternity itself, it won't matter how many members have come to sit and soak, memorizing Bible verses and absorbing doctrine. What will matter is if we've neglected those who are crying and hurting within our walls. If we've done that, we'll have failed as a body of servant-believers. Paul anxiously hopes that the Philippians will avoid such devastating failure.

The apostle goes on to tell his readers how they can avoid missing the mark. He urges them to be "of the same mind" (2:2). That involves, according to Paul, thinking the same thoughts and having the same love (2:2). It means avoiding selfish actions and empty self-glorification (2:3). It demands placing the interests of others above one's own (2:3-4). It necessitates adopting, as much as is humanly possible, the mind of Christ (2:5).

THE MIND OF CHRIST

To paraphrase Dallas Cowboys head coach Tom Landry, "When a man thinks right, he'll act right. When he's right in the head, he'll be right on the field." The apostle Paul might have said essentially the same thing. He certainly recognized the fact that if the minds of the Philippians were like the mind of Christ, then their conduct would take care of itself.

What is that mind of Christ? How does that mind think? What decisions does that mind make in light of the thoughts that it thinks? We'll find answers to these questions as we consider the next six verses of Philippians 2. We'll be stepping behind the stage to see what precipitated the incarnation—the coming of Jesus to dwell among us in bodily form. The vision we'll see is of a compassionate Christ who considered the cost, who permitted Himself to be cradled in Bethlehem and offered up at Calvary. We'll examine His attitudes and His actions, subject matter well worthy of our Christmas meditation as we celebrate His coming.

Existing in the Form of God

Paul tells us in Philippians 2:6 that Christ is He who is existing "in the form of God." The Greek word for *form* is *morphe,* signifying an unchanging essence. No surrender can be made on this point: Jesus Christ is God almighty! Christ's essence, His changeless being, is divine. He did not give up His Godhood when He came to earth as a babe in Bethlehem.

There is a great deal of misunderstanding throughout the church world on this issue. Liberals often latch onto the idea that when Christ became a tiny baby, He ceased to be God. He grew to manhood and became a great moral teacher. He was a shining example for us to follow, yes, but a strictly human example at that, and we can be just like Him if we try hard enough. The problem with that is that the Bible says something different.

The Scriptures tell us that Christ is God. His human appearance enabled those who knew Him to touch Him, to see Him, to dine with Him, to walk alongside Him. His humanity permitted Him to be "tempted in every way, just as we are," yet His deity ensured that He remained "without sin" (Hebrews 4:15 NIV). It was absolutely essential that

Christ, in order to fulfill the divine requirements of the justice of God and bring about the redemption of mankind, be clothed in human flesh while remaining wholly God. He was and is and always shall be a portion of the Trinity: God the Father, the Son, and the Holy Spirit. Anyone who denies the divinity of Jesus cannot truly know Him as Savior and Lord.

Christ could not have been merely a great moral teacher. If that were the case, then some of the statements He made would have to be considered outright lies. Great moral teachers try not to lie, and they certainly don't allow their lies to be recorded for all posterity!

Jesus claimed to be God. "I and the Father are one," He succinctly states in John 10:30 (NASB). "He who has seen Me has seen the Father," He admonishes Philip in John 14:9 (NASB). Christ also claimed to have been in existence eternally. "Truly, truly, I say to you, before Abraham was born, I am," He tells a group of Jews in John 8:58 (NASB). In other words, He says that He was alive before Abraham was ever born. Was Jesus simply a liar? No, indeed! He was and is very God.

Others surely saw it that way. Let's look at some of the statements made about Christ by His contemporaries. First, let's look at the words of His friends:

> Simon Peter: "Thou art the Christ, the Son of the living God" (Matthew 16:16 NASB).
> The disciples: "And those who were in the boat worshiped Him, saying, 'You are certainly God's Son!'" (Matthew 14:33 NASB).
> Mark: "The beginning of the gospel about Jesus Christ, the Son of God" (Mark 1:1 NIV).
> John the Baptist: "I have seen and I testify that this is the Son of God" (John 1:34 NIV).
> Nathaniel: "Rabbi, you are the Son of God; you are the King of Israel" (John 1:49 NIV).

Martha: "Yes, Lord; I have believed that you are
the Christ, the Son of God, who was to come
into the world" (John 11:27 NIV).
Thomas: "My Lord and my God!" (John 20:28 NASB).
Paul: "He is the Son of God" (Acts 9:20 NASB).

Now, what about His foes, those who either actively
fought against Him or who represented His enemies?

The unclean spirits: "And whenever the unclean
spirits beheld Him, they would fall down before
Him and cry out, saying, 'You are the Son of
God!' " (Mark 3:11 NASB).
A man demon-possessed: "What do I have to do with
You, Jesus, Son of the Most High?" (Mark 5:7
NASB).
A Roman centurion: "Truly this man was the Son of
God!" (Mark 15:39 NASB).

God the Father Himself said it at the moment Jesus began
His public ministry. After Christ had been baptized by John
the Baptist, the Spirit of God in the form of a dove descended
upon Him from the heavens. The thundering voice of God
proclaimed, "This is My beloved Son, in whom I am well-
pleased" (Matthew 3:17 NASB). Truly Jesus is God the Son.
Any other explanation cannot account for the eyewitnesses
who knew it to be so. Believe me, they had nothing to gain
by proclaiming Christ's deity. Many, such as Stephen, Paul,
James the son of Zebedee, and John the Baptist, suffered
martyrs' deaths, yet they would not deny the truth, for they
were convinced of His claims.

Besides, Jesus' deeds showed Him to be God. He told a
crippled man to take up his bed and walk, and a blind beggar
to wash in the pool of Siloam and see. A woman who had
suffered for years with a hemorrhage was cured the instant

she touched the hem of His garment. He filled the nets of fishermen to the bursting point. He calmed a stormy sea with, "Peace, be still." He walked across water, saying, "Take courage! It is I. Don't be afraid" (Mark 6:50 NIV). He roused the daughter of a prominent Roman official from the dead, and in a graveyard He called His friend Lazarus forth from the tomb. He Himself broke the bans of death that first Easter morning. Who else save God could have done all of this? Make no mistake about it, that little baby of Bethlehem was God in human flesh!

YIELDING HIS POSITION

Jesus exists in the form of God. And yet as Paul goes on to tell his readers in Philippians 2:6, Christ "considered not this being equal with God something to cling to." He willingly gave up His dwelling place with the Father in heaven to be born in blood and tears in an imperfect world. When the time came for His coming, Jesus could have said, "No! I don't want to go! Find somebody else! Send an angel instead!" But He didn't. Motivated by love, He permitted Himself to be shrouded in flesh for thirty-three years.

In that time, His life was the epitome of humility. When Salome, the mother of James and John, asked Jesus to place her sons at His side in His kingdom, Christ informed the twelve:

> Whoever wishes to become great among you shall be your servant, and whoever wishes to be first among you shall be your slave; just as the Son of Man did not come to be served, but to serve, and to give His life a ransom for many (Matthew 20:26-28 NASB).

During His tenure on earth, Jesus owned nothing of what we might call material wealth. He had to borrow a place in which to be born, a house in which to sleep, a boat from which to preach, a donkey on which to ride, a room in which to eat His last supper, and a tomb in which to be buried. Not only did God's Son become poor in adopting human appearance, but by human standards He was homeless, hungry, and poverty-stricken. "The foxes have holes, and the birds of the air have nests; but the Son of Man has nowhere to lay His head," He said to a scribe who offered to follow Him (Matthew 8:20 NASB).

The verb *cling* used in Philippians 2:6 suggests the idea of a treasure to be retained at any price. Residence in heaven is an unimaginable treasure which none would give up. None, that is, except God the Son, who surrendered His "rights" for the purpose of saving sinners.

Coming to Calvary

As Jesus temporarily traded the sparkling mansions of heaven for the dusty hovels of the world, His journey was one of increasing humility, unto the greatest humiliation of them all: the cross. As Paul writes in Philippians 2:7-8, Jesus "emptied Himself, having taken the form of a servant, becoming in the likeness of men. And being found fashioned as a man, He humbled Himself, having become obedient even to death, the death of the cross." Let's look more closely at the stages of our Lord's humiliation.

He Emptied Himself

First, Christ emptied Himself. He did not empty Himself of His Godhood or His deity, but He, as the King James Bible puts it, "made himself of no reputation." He was willing to take on human flesh. He was willing to surrender divine prerogatives. He was willing to suffer hunger, thirst, temptation, harrassment, so that He might become our faithful, understanding high priest. Hymnist Emily Elliott put it this way:

Thou didst leave Thy throne and Thy kingly crown
When Thou camest to earth for me;
But in Bethlehem's home was there found no room
For Thy holy nativity.

Heaven's arches rang when the angels sang,
Proclaiming Thy royal decree;
But in lowly birth didst Thou come to earth,
And in great humility.

He Came as a Servant

Not only did Jesus empty Himself, but He also took on the form of a servant. Mark 10:45 says: "For even the Son of Man did not come to be served, but to serve, and to give His life a ransom for many" (NASB).

After the cross, probably the next classic example of Christ's servanthood occurs when He is in the upper room with His disciples: a group of men with dirty feet. The disciples are very "religious," yet too proud to grab towels and start washing. It is Jesus who redefines greatness and power and love by wrapping a towel around His waist and pouring water into a basin, then gently washing the dirt and dust from the feet of His followers. He does this even though He is fully aware that the hour of His suffering is ominously close at hand (John 13:1-16).

He Was Fashioned as a Man

Christ emptied Himself; He came as a servant, and He also allowed Himself to be fashioned as a man, according to Paul. It was no coincidence that He was born through a virgin's womb, that He arrived as a tiny baby with all the limitations of physical humanity. It was an absolute necessity. Born in abject poverty and obscurity to a peasant maid, the Christ came—a man of sorrows, acquainted with grief. He had to be made like us, so that we might be made like Him.

He Humbled Himself

All of the things Christ did in emptying Himself, in taking on human flesh, in performing as a servant, necessitated that He humble Himself. And this He did.

He subjected Himself to the authority of Mary and Joseph in His early years. Though the creator of the universe, He became a simple carpenter. He patiently waited thirty years before beginning His public ministry. He kept company with mere fishermen, not kings or princes. He allowed Himself to be betrayed for a few pieces of silver. He submitted to crucifixion—an excruciating execution from which Roman citizens were exempted because it was considered too degrading.

He Was Obedient unto Death

It is amazing to realize that Christ willingly gave His life for us! Death is something we all resist. As I look out into my congregations, I see handfuls of men and women who battle death daily. Their bodies riddled with cancer or weakened by heart disease, they keep fighting the fight. Sunday after surprising Sunday they make it to the sanctuary. They're Christians; they're not afraid to die. But they are not willing to be obedient unto death!

Christ, in all humility, had to set aside His life. But don't think that He eagerly anticipated physical death. He dreaded it, but He accepted it.

John 13:1 states that "Jesus knew that the time had come for him to leave this world and go to the Father" (NIV). His hour had come. Aware of this, Christ left the upper room. Flanked by disciples He knew would fail Him, He marched through the Kidron Valley to the garden of Gethsemane. There He prayed, "Father, if it is possible, let this cup pass from Me; yet not as I will, but as Thou wilt" (Matthew 26:39 NASB). You see, He really didn't relish the idea of dying! And yet to the cross He went.

Calvary was the ultimate humiliation. When Christ proclaimed, "Father, into Thy hands I commit My spirit" (Luke 23:46 NASB), and gave up His Spirit, He signaled the end of a life marked by full, complete, willing obedience to the Father, an obedience even unto death. That is humility. That is self-sacrifice. That is our Savior who, as 1 Peter 2:24 states, "bore our sins in His body on the cross, that we might die to sin and live to righteousness" (NASB).

Closing Thoughts

In a world filled with the me-first mentality, how refreshing it is to read of the humility of the King of kings! This Christmas, let's ask the Lord to work in us so that we might become more transparently humble. Let's pray for chances to be servants. Let's carefully watch for opportunities to place the interests of others above our own. Here are a few suggestions:

1. Focus in your family on what you can do for others, rather than yourselves. As a family, adopt somebody—say, an elderly widow or a lonely college student—for the holidays. Invite someone extra to share in the festivities of your home and hearth.
2. Grab a towel and serve the members of your own family in tangible ways this Christmas. This means more than volunteering to dry the dishes after the the big meal, although that might be a good place to start.
3. Do something for someone else that is really going to cost you in terms of time, involvement, and mon-

ey. The possibilities are endless—use your imagination!

Let's keep in mind two thoughts. First, remember that "as a man thinketh in his heart, so is he" (Proverbs 23:7 KJV). Second, remember the mind of Christ and the attitudes which resulted in actions of service, by which He showed us His transcending love. The words to Kate Wilkinson's immortal hymn offer a challenge to us all.

> May the mind of Christ, my Savior,
> Live in me from day to day,
> By His love and pow'r controlling
> All I do and say.

Do you want to change the world this Christmas? Then make this resolution: determine to ask God to show you how to be a servant for His sake. Believe me, He won't disappoint you!

Reflections for the season

1. To be effective as a servant, you must think of the needs of others first.

2. Are you trying to see the face of Christ in those people with whom you differ?

3. Words of encouragement and affirmation can be a real ministry.

4. Make a list of people with whom you desire to fellowship and begin praying for them.

The Greatest Giver
2 Corinthians 9:6-15

*C*hristmas is the season for giving and receiving. It usually works this way: parents give; kids receive . . . at least when the children are young!

I think it must have been a man with several children who first made the observation that Christmas is the time when both money and kids sprout wings. My experience with our brood of five has definitely reinforced this theory. Each December, checkbooks and wallets do shrinking acts, while ordinarily rambunctious, messy, semi-well-mannered kids adopt behaviors bordering, for them, on the wing-sprouting angelic. Brothers and sisters declare cease-fires on arguments. They clean their rooms without being reminded twenty times. They open doors for people over thirty. As the 25th draws near, they even offer to help with the dishes. It's amazing! And it works. Santa Claus is coming to town!

In return, we moms and dads determine to give our best to the obedient little guys and gals by making their Christmas morning memorable. "What do you want Santa to bring you?" we voice frequently as we aspire to please. We rise to the occasion and try not to disappoint, even if it involves sacrifice on our part.

SACRIFICING FOR THE SEASON

I can remember some pretty slim Christmases from our seminary days and years of early ministry. Yet Pearl and I always tried to please our children with gifts that surprised and satisfied because they knew we had sacrificed. One year, one of our children desperately yearned for a bicycle, but we could not see our way clear to buy one. Guess what happened? Some friends gave us a bike which their kids had outgrown! With the help of a solid scrubbing and a can of red spray paint, that bicycle looked like it had just come off the showroom floor when we rolled it under the tree on Christmas morning! There is a special joy in that kind of giving. It is letting the child see that the real giver is his heavenly Father.

Yes, parents do sacrifice to make Christmas extra-special for their families. It doesn't take long for the new to wear off, the toys to break, and things to get back to normal, but we still scrimp, save, and spend, preparing for December 25. And to be honest, we often overdo things.

More than once I have reclined in the easy chair after doing my part in polishing off a huge Christmas dinner with turkey and all the trimmings, only to be interrupted in my relaxing (read that, digesting) by thoughts of the morning's massive gift exchange. At such times I have frequently wondered if all the folderol was justifiable. Sometimes it seemed we had all focused too much on the material. Sometimes there was just a gnawing feeling of emptiness—the kind which turkey and dressing won't fill—which made me ask the question, "Is that all there is?"

The Christmas of No Regrets

As a family, we've found a few methods to avoid the emptiness. First, we've determined not to go completely overboard in our gift-giving. We don't give everything to everybody, and nobody receives ultra-expensive, frivolous items.

We've also found that looking again at the Christmas story in Luke 2 is good medicine for an attack of the overkill syndrome. Our Lord was born into incredibly modest circumstances. The first Christmas Day was by no means a material extravaganza, but a simple time of honest worship and praise. Since God Himself chose to cloak His coming in all humility and simplicity, do we really have to turn our celebrations of Christmas into occasions of enormous indulgence?

And before we do exchange presents in our family, we consciously refresh ourselves about the reasons why we are doing it. Our gift-giving then becomes an object lesson to remind us that God is the greatest giver of them all, having given us His Son. Talk about sacrificing for the season! God did not skimp with us in His choice of a Christmas present. He gave us the very best: a priceless possession, Jesus Christ. I'm not suggesting that the Lord overdid things, either. The gift of Christ was just right. Nothing else could have sufficed to remove the stain of sin from the hearts of men. And no greater sacrifice has ever been made than the one which had its earthly beginnings on that first Christmas Day.

It's Our Serve

How then, do we properly respond to the season of giving? In our last chapter, we discussed the healthy benefits of service for Christ's sake. Now we're going to take that discussion a step farther.

You see, God has not just given us His Son, though Jesus

would be gift enough for anyone. He has also been gracious to give each of us specific kinds of talents, quantities of time, and certain amounts of money. What we do with these talents, time, and money is something called *stewardship*. Since Christmas is the season of giving, maybe it's time we pause and see how we're doing. What kind of stewards are we? Openhanded or closefisted? Stingy or straightforward?

Please be warned: this chapter is not an argument for tithing. It's not designed to make you grudgingly dip into your pockets for donations or grumpily scratch room on your already-full calendars for hours of service. Instead, I hope it provides food for thought on what God would have you to do with the tangible things He has given you. I pray that you'll be driven to ask the Lord to show you opportunities for the effective stewardship of your resources. I also hope that you will be freed from the effects of some of the teaching on giving which openly or subtly deviates from scriptural truth.

Let's turn now to one of the greatest passages on stewardship in the Scriptures: 2 Corinthians 9:6-15. There the apostle Paul begins with advice on wise giving and ends with an outburst of praise to the greatest giver of them all. Shall we see what he has to say to us?

> Now this I am saying, he who is sowing sparingly shall also reap sparingly, and he who is sowing bountifully shall also reap bountifully.
> Let each one give just as he has purposed in his heart, not grudgingly or under compulsion, for God is loving a cheerful giver.
> And God is able to make all grace abound to you in order that, having always enough of everything, you may have an abundance for every good deed.
> Even as it stands written, He scattered abroad, He gave to those who are poor, His righteousness is abiding forever.

Now He who is supplying seed to the sower and bread for food will supply and multiply your seed for sowing and increase the harvest of your righteousness.

You, being enriched in everything for all generosity, which through us is producing thanksgiving to God.

Because the ministry of this service is not only fully supplying the needs of the saints but also is overflowing through many thanksgivings to God.

Because of the approved character of your service, they are glorifying God for your obedience to your confession of the gospel of Christ and the generosity of your contribution to them and to all,

While they also with petitions on your behalf are longing for you because of the extraordinary grace of God in you.

Thanks be to God for His indescribable gift.

OF TOUGH TIMES

The January, 1987, issue of *Texas Monthly* magazine aptly described 1986 on its cover as, "The Year That Went Belly-Up." If you're familiar with our Texas economy these days, you know just how disturbingly true that assessment is. In '86, real-estate development stood still. Vast office buildings stood empty. The oil industry barely managed to stand at all. And just about every Texan stood in disbelief at the crumbling financial state of the state.

At the time Paul writes 2 Corinthians 9:6-15, there is an economic crisis of sorts going on in Jerusalem, too—only its principle victims are Christians. Many of the members of the Jerusalem church are practically destitute. Persecution has driven scores from their homes. There is a shortage of food and shelter. They are desperately in need of assistance.

In his missionary journeys, Paul had traveled to many places, including the city of Corinth in Greece. To these Gentile believers, he had evidently communicated news of the difficulties which the believers in Jerusalem were experiencing, and had elicited a promise of material help. But, apparently, no gift from the Corinthians had been sent as yet to the Jerusalem church. So Paul saves space in his letter to remind the Christians at Corinth of their obligation.

He tactfully brings up the subject of giving by first referring to the generosity of the Macedonians, who had given liberally despite their own deep poverty (see 8:1-3). These Christians, needy themselves, had literally begged Paul for the opportunity to contribute to the aid of the saints in Jerusalem (8:4). The heart of the matter was that the Macedonians had completely committed themselves to the Lord. Their generosity was an outgrowth of this heartfelt compassion and dedication (8:5).

Following this convicting example, Paul goes on to remind the Corinthians of God's own generosity with believers. He gives the example of the One who was rich and became poor for our sakes. Writes the apostle, "For you know the grace of our Lord Jesus Christ, that though He was rich, yet for your sake He became poor, that you through His poverty might become rich" (8:9 NASB). What better illustration could Paul have chosen than our Lord? He descended from the heavenly places into the pit of poverty, giving of Himself completely for our well being.

As chapter 9 of 2 Corinthians opens, Paul continues his discourse on giving. Let's pick up his message in verses 6 through 15. There we'll consider the *principles* of giving (9:6-8), the *promise* of giving (9:9-10), the *provision* of giving (9:11-13), the *potential* for giving (9:14), and, finally, the glorious *picture* of it all (9:15). Please, read on.

THE PRINCIPLES OF GIVING—2 CORINTHIANS 9:6-8

In reality, the gospel of our Lord Jesus Christ is founded on the principle and grounded in the spirit of giving. There is no buying or selling of the gospel—God does not barter and bargain with us. In grace He gives us everything: Jesus, eternal life, His Spirit, His glory. As New Testament believers, our own giving should be the result of hearts which have been touched by the grace of God. Freely we have received; now freely we should count it as a privilege to be able to give of our energies, time, talents, and resources.

When a man's heart has been touched by love, there often is nothing which will keep him from sacrificing his interests for the sake of his loved one. There is ecstasy in giving the best we have to the one we love most. So should it be with our giving to God.

OUR CHOICE—TO SOW, NOT TO SOW, HOW MUCH TO SOW?

In verse 6 of 2 Corinthians 9, Paul shares with us principles of giving. In verse 7, we see the apostle's command, and in verse 8, the response of God. Writes Paul, "Now this I am saying, he who is sowing sparingly shall also reap sparingly and he who is sowing bountifully shall also reap bountifully" (9:6).

The images mentioned in verse 6 call to mind a picture of a garden, of sowing and reaping. The verse also suggests the first principle of stewardship: *Giving is not charity; it is an investment.* If we put something in, we'll be getting something out. If we sow, we shall reap (see also Galatians 6:7-9). As Proverbs 19:17 puts it, "He who is gracious to a poor man lends to the LORD, And He will repay him for his good deed" (NASB). And Proverbs 11:25 teaches that "the generous man will be prosperous, And he who waters will himself be watered" (NASB).

Don't make the mistake of assuming that the return on your investment will necessarily be material, either. God isn't always in the business of showering us with big bucks. The principle of "seed faith" so popular with certain evangelists these days is the product of a tragic misunderstanding and manipulation of the biblical text for selfish reasons. How

narrow it is to limit the idea of prosperity to material benefits, when God's blessings encompass so much more.

In God's sight, the giving heart is a heart that is making
an investment. The amount of the investment is up to us.
Notice that verse 6 contains a statement of choice. We can
either sow "sparingly" or "bountifully." And thus we encoun-
ter principle number two: *The amount and type of our
giving is strictly between us and the Lord.* It's our decision.
That may surprise some of us who have been brought up on
the pledge card and the tithe, but giving is scripturally a
personal matter. It's business between you and God. It should
not be the stuff of fundraising campaigns and public con-
tracts. The pressure to give exerted even by Christian organizations can be appalling. I believe that for the Lord's work,
done the Lord's way, the Lord will provide.

Just look at the command Paul gives his readers in verse
7: "Let each one give just as he has purposed in his heart,
not grudgingly or under compulsion, for God is loving a
cheerful giver." Does Paul make mention of a mandatory
tithe? Does the text read, "Let each one tithe just as he has
purposed in his heart . . ."? No! Historically, we see the tithe
in the Old Testament but once, when Abraham paid a tithe to
Melchizedek (Genesis 14:20). Jesus later speaks of tithing in
a rather derogatory fashion in the New Testament (see Matthew 23:23-24; Matthew 6:1-4). As a Jew, the apostle Paul
could well have instituted such mandatory giving within the
early church, but he speaks nothing of it.

When you get down to it, the gospel of our Lord is
amazingly free and exciting. In speaking in Romans 14 of
our Christian conduct, Paul doesn't lay guilt on us about
adhering to a list of yeses and noes. Instead, he urges us,
"Let each man be fully convinced in his own mind" about the
rightness or wrongness of actions (14:5b NASB). Don't mis-
read me—there are scriptural absolutes of moral and immor-
al behavior. Yet in the "gray" situations, what we permit in
our lives and what we don't permit in our lives is between the

Father and us. We shall reap what we sow. The same is true for our giving.

We are exhorted in 2 Corinthians 9:7 to give as we purpose in our hearts. We're free to invest as the Lord leads us. These are the principles of giving. Yet there are guidelines we must follow as we give. As verse 7 also says, we must not give "grudgingly" or "under compulsion."

Giving "grudgingly" and "under compulsion" means plopping our checks in the collection plate and muttering to ourselves, "I don't want to give this, but I've got to." If that is your attitude, friend, let me give you some advice.

First, consider what God has done for you. If He hasn't done anything for you, then don't give Him a dime. He doesn't want your money unless you know Him as Savior, and if you think He hasn't done anything for you, then your salvation is open to question, to say the least.

Something else to remember is this: God doesn't need our money! He doesn't . . . but *we* need to give it to Him. He doesn't need our time or talents, either, but we need to let Him use them. And, according to verse 7, we need to do so cheerfully!

"God is loving a cheerful giver," encourages Paul. In this instance, the word *cheerful* means "hilarious." In other words, God loves a cheerful, joyful, abundant, excited giver! He wants us to be happy about our giving—thrilled with the anticipation of it. He has certainly been a cheerful giver Himself. Remember how gleefully the angel announced the birth of the Messiah to the shepherds in the field? "Do not be afraid; for behold, I bring you good news of a great joy which shall be for all the people," proclaimed Gabriel (Luke 2:10). And it is written that Jesus "for the *joy* set before Him endured the cross" (Hebrews 12:2 NASB, italics mine). Giving Himself for us was an act of sheer ecstasy for our Lord!

Though He did not relish the idea of a painful physical death, He was glad to sacrifice Himself for our sakes.

God loves a cheerful giver . . . and He hates a dishonest one. In Acts 5, Ananias and Sapphira found that out the hard way. They sold a piece of property and pretended to give all the proceeds to the church. In reality they kept a portion of the profits for themselves. Their lying didn't fool the Holy Spirit and their lives were instantaneously snuffed out (see 5:1-10). They were not judged because they did not give the whole amount promised, but because they lied about it, giving the impression that they were giving all when they weren't. They definitely weren't cheerful givers, and they reaped dust, death, and dishonor in return.

How do you give? Examine yourself on that one. Are you free with your time in serving others? Do you give of your talents and abilities? Do you give of yourself as a teacher of God's Word, in leading Bible studies or instructing your children? And, although it is the easiest way out because there is no lingering responsibility once the bank balance is sound, do you give of your money? Are you cheerful about it?

With gratitude I reflect on the many, many members of our congregations who donate six to eight hours several times a year to help our staff put out the Ministries' 8000 quarterly newsletters. How cheerful and excited everyone is to be involved in the process! Each instance is a lighthearted, happy occasion . . . and that is what God loves.

THE RESULTS ARE UP TO HIM

We've seen the principles that giving is productive, an investment, that we reap what we sow. We've also discussed that giving is personal. We decide what sort of crop we want, what kind of garden we'll put in. It's a matter of choice, business between the Lord and us. In verse 8, Paul assures us that it will be God who prospers and blesses our efforts. In the apostle's words: "And God is able to make all grace abound to you in order that, having always enough of every-thing, you may have an abundance for every good deed." God abundantly grants us His grace. Why? So that we might be able to respond to the opportunities He gives us to pro-vide for others.

In Genesis 39, the Bible states that the Lord blessed every-thing that Joseph did, and that He prospered everything which came into his hands (see 39:5,23). Blessing, prosper-ity, ability, talent—all these come from the Lord. When we scatter our resources, God prospers our sowing. The harvest of fruit is His, and He ensures that we have enough seed for the crops.

My parents' garden is a good illustration of this. I believe that my folks extended their lives a good bit by acquiring some acreage and planting a   large vegetable garden. It was always a joy to go there in season, especially since my own gardens rarely survive through the June Texas heat. Mom and Dad were known for annually hauling in bumper crops of peas, potatoes, cabbage, beans, cauliflower, corn, cucum-bers, squash, and tomatoes. Even though their garden was never big by garden standards, their freezer was overflow-ing by the end of summer. They had tomatoes all over the place and potatoes piled up everywhere. My mom made a career of fixing squash a thousand different ways (though squash sandwiches were a bit hard to swallow). And with every passing year, when things began to ripen, my folks started giving. They gave away so much produce that they must have kept ten families in vegetables. No matter how much they passed out, God just kept prospering that garden. There was always more than enough. That's the way He works. He provides, so that we can provide for others.

Jesus Himself says in Luke 6:38, "Give, and it will be given to you. A good measure, pressed down, shaken togeth-er and running over, will be poured into your lap. For with the measure you use, it will be measured to you" (NIV). As John Bunyan puts it in his classic *Pilgrim's Progress,* "A man there was though some did count him mad, The more he cast away, the more he had." And King Solomon, the wealthiest man of his day, writes in Ecclesiastes 11:1, "Cast your bread upon the waters, for after many days you will find it again" (NIV).

Does this mean that we'll be wealthy if we are generous in giving? Not necessarily. God never promises to make us all rich. In the Bible, it is true that there are some very well-to-do men like Abraham, Jacob, Solomon, and Joseph. Yet the apostles were not men of means, neither were countless others. The Lord promises to supply our needs, that is all. What verse 8 tells us is that He is able to provide for us through His grace, that we might in turn give to others. He is able to prosper us. He can do it . . . but the doing is entirely up to Him. And just because God might not have given us vast financial resources does not mean that we should not give what we can and how we can.

THE PROMISE OF GIVING—2 CORINTHIANS 9:9-10

We've discussed the principles of giving. We've seen in verse 8 what God is able to do for us. Now, in 2 Corinthians 9:9-10, we'll see what God will do for us as we give. Let's look at the promise of giving. Writes Paul:

> Even as it stands written, He scattered abroad, He gave to those who are poor, His righteousness is abiding forever.
> Now He who is supplying seed to the sower and bread for food will supply and multiply your seed for sowing and increase the harvest of your righteousness.

Not only is God able to supply our needs, *He will do so.* The text says that He will supply seed for sowing; He will multiply that seed; He will increase the harvest. Again, I emphasize the fact that we may not become wealthy. Certainly I've never been bothered with the burden of excess cash! But the Lord will provide enough for us and enough to give.

How does He do it? As Donald Grey Barnhouse once replied when asked how the Lord could have sustained two million Israelites wandering in the desert for forty years, "Only one word, Sir. GOD." He can do it because He is God.

We shouldn't find this hard to believe. It was the Lord who took five small loaves and a few fish from the lunch bucket of a little boy, and turned it into a meal for five thousand plus, with twelve basketfuls left over (John 6:5-13).

This year we celebrate the fifteenth anniversary of Don Anderson Ministries, and we have only survived because of the grace and provision of God. We have never taken an offering at a Bible class or even initiated letting our financial needs be known, but the Lord has met every single expense. The bills are paid for this month. He knows what we'll need in the bank for next month and He has always been faithful to provide. We just go on—holding the camps and conferences, teaching the Bible classes, ministering at two churches, producing tapes, books, and newsletters, involving ourselves in the lives of people who are hurting—and He takes care of the rest.

How does God do it? I don't know, but He is able, and when He sees the giving heart, He will supply, multiply, and increase the sowing and the harvest. That is His promise.

THE PROVISION: WHAT GIVING GIVES—2 CORINTHIANS 9:11-13

Paul goes on to tell his readers what the act of giving itself will give to them. Giving does something for the giver, it does something for the receiver, and it does something for God! Let's read on.

"You," writes the apostle, "being enriched in everything for all generosity, which through us is producing thanksgiving to God" (9:11). The giver is enriched by the act of giving! Being generous generates an awfully good feeling in our hearts! And this good feeling produces thanksgiving to God. We become grateful to Him for allowing us to constructively contribute to the lives of others.

Then, in verse 12, Paul reveals what giving does for the receiver: "Because the ministry of this service is not only fully supplying the needs of the saints but also is overflowing through many thanksgivings to God." It goes without saying that receivers receive what givers give. Giving ensures that needs are met, yet those who receive wind up with far more than just the things they lack. Receivers also experience the enriching feeling of being grateful to God. They tangibly see His power and love working through others. And again, thanks directed toward God overflow when this kind of generous giving occurs.

What does the Lord receive from acts of giving done in His name? Paul answers that in verse 13: "Because of the approved character of your service, they are glorifying God for your obedience to your confession of the gospel of Christ and the generosity of your contribution to them and to all." It's simple; what God gets is glory. He is glorified when we give, because we are being obedient to His wishes. Our Christianity is seen by the onlooking world to be authentic. Our light comes out from under the bushel and brightly shines as we are generous. Perhaps others even come to know Christ as Savior because they have seen that He motivates us to do great good for His glory.

THE POTENTIAL OF GIVING—2 CORINTHIANS 9:14

There is tremendous *potential* in giving, as well. Paul writes the Corinthians that the Christians in Jerusalem "also, with petitions on your behalf, are longing for you because of the extraordinary grace of God in you" (9:14). The suffering saints are so grateful for the promised generosity of their fellow believers in Corinth that they pray for them, making "petitions" on their behalf. Not only that, but the Jerusalem

Christians also long to visit the Corinthians, to get to know them because of their loving contributions and their obvious love of God.

Basically, the members of the church in Jerusalem, who are mostly Christian Jews, probably are astonished that Greek Gentiles whom they have never met are supporting them as brothers in God's family. The receivers are thinking to themselves, these Corinthians are really special. God's grace abounds in them. We'd like to have the opportunity to meet these men and women, but at least we can pray for them. And they do.

Today we have opportunities to support missionaries stationed anywhere from inner-city ghettos to jungles in Ecuador to seminaries in Belgium. I hope that your church and you as an individual have the vision to contribute to missionaries of your choice. They are our representatives in the harvest fields of the world. We make their ministries possible by our sacrificial giving. May God enlarge our perspectives to realize that these missionaries, in turn, are going to pray for us, even as we meet their needs. They'll make petitions to the Lord on our behalf and they'll long to come see us, because we are brothers and sisters with the same heavenly Father, laborers together.

THE PICTURE OF GIVING—*2 CORINTHIANS 9:15*

In case you're wondering where the Christmas message is in this chapter, here it is. In verse 15, Paul bursts forth with an incredibly beautiful and emotional doxology, "Thanks be to God for His indescribable gift." While many feel that Paul refers to the gifts of the Gentiles with that statement, I think he means much more. I believe that he speaks of the greatest giver of them all.

Are you a giver? God is a giver too, and you'll never outgive Him. It isn't possible, and here is the picture of it all.

God's giving defies description. Paul knows no word which

will convey the richness of His provision for us, so he labels it as "indescribable." We are speechless at two times in our lives: when we are overwhelmed with gratitude, and when we are stricken with grief. It is with immense gratitude and intense grief that we should respond to the gift of God at Calvary.

Even a man of words and letters like the apostle could not utter adjectives adequate to describe what God has done for His children. Yet throughout his writings, he urges his readers to respond with gratitude at God's giving. He prays that the Christians at Ephesus might have their capacities enlarged so that they could comprehend the height, depth, width, and breadth of the love of God in Christ Jesus (Ephesians 3:18-19). In 1 Corinthians 15:57, he exclaims, "But thanks be to God! He gives us the victory through our Lord Jesus Christ" (NIV). In Romans 11:33, he cries, "Oh, the depth of the riches both of the wisdom and knowledge of God! How unsearchable are His judgments and unfathomable His ways!" God's ways are a marvelous mystery, worthy of our highest praise and our unending gratitude.

Thinking of all that the Lord has given us should also bring tears to our eyes. We should grieve at the thought of what He has endured for our sakes. Like Mary and the women at the cross, we should weep at the thought of Calvary. Sending His beloved Son to that cross was His greatest gift to a sinful humanity thus far.

At the Cross, at the Cross

Why did God create the human race in the first place? He did so because He was lonely, because He wanted a relationship, because He wanted someone to love. Rather than settling for an chiefly inanimate world incapable of returning His affection, He formed man and woman.

Because our parents didn't do too good a job in the garden, the Lord found Himself picking up the pieces of broken humanity. It was time for Plan B. The love of the greatest lover would have to give all that was necessary to restore the fallen relationship between man and his maker. Only God could bind the broken hearts and deal with the problem of sin. Immediately He made plans for the giving of His own Son as a promised seed. He entered into a covenant relationship with Abraham.

Hundreds of years later, God came down through the heavens, past the stellar spaces, to a little clod of dirt called Bethlehem. Almighty God left His scepter and crown to assume the appearance of a man. Who can comprehend a love and commitment like that? For thirty-three years He wandered about, well acquainted with sorrow, no stranger to grief.

And then there was the cross. I believe that all the world and even the angels were silent as God the Father turned His back while God the Son split the air waves with the orphaned cry, "My God, My God, why hast Thou forsaken Me?" (Matthew 27:46 NASB). Blackness engulfed the earth, and in those hours, He bore the crushing weight of our sins. As if that weren't gift enough, the Lord then sent His Spirit to dwell within us, a comforter and a conscience.

God's desire is to make us like His Son, yet how many times we thwart His purpose. Still He, with patient forgiveness, continues the slow, painful process in our lives of making us Christlike. He creates us for that relationship. He purchased it with the blood of His Son.

BEYOND THE CROSS

Words fail us when we try to fathom God's immeasurable sacrifice, His ultimate gift. But you know, He has still another gift in store for those of us who call Him Savior and Lord. Someday we shall, in the words of 1 Peter 1:4, "obtain an inheritance which is imperishable and undefiled and will not fade away, reserved in heaven" for us (NASB).

"In My Father's house are many dwelling places; if it were not so, I would have told you; for I go to prepare a place for you," says Jesus in John 14:2 (NASB). He loves us so much that He has gone to get our eternal residence ready. It is a Christmas present He has been working on for nearly two thousand years now. All of the earthly blessings we experience are but the down payment, the interest on the inheritance. The real stuff is coming, when we arrive in His presence through death or the rapture. And it will be an incredible gift. "Eye hath not seen, nor ear heard, neither have entered into the heart of man, the things which God hath prepared for them that love him" (1 Corinthians 2:9 KJV).

Perhaps you're thinking, all that may be well and good, but I am lonely *today.* I believe that in many ways, God strips us down while we are on the earth, so that we'll get homesick for heaven. Maybe that is happening to you. If you know Christ as Savior, then you possess His Spirit. You are not alone. Lean on Him. One day you will behold His beauty face to face. Onward to the prize before you!

The Tragedy of Christmas

Grandpa and Grandma, Mom and Dad, your children and grandchildren, operate on very limited financial resources. But it's Christmas time, and for the past six months, they've been planning a gift for you. They've been mowing lawns, raking leaves, doing the dishes, and hauling out the garbage. The other day, they got your special present out of layaway. Now it's wrapped in red paper and resting under the tree, and they're counting the hours till you open the gift.

Christmas morning comes . . . and what is your response to the carefully planned present? Do you say, "I'm sorry, I don't like it. It's unsuitable. Please return it." Of course you don't! You'd never do that, would you? And yet perhaps you have done that very thing with the gospel of Christ.

In essence, you've told God, "I'm sorry, but Jesus doesn't

fit. I can't wear the gift of Christ in public. He'll take away my joy." Perish the thought. Christ waits beneath God's Christmas tree, the cross, to give you eternal life and a relationship with Him.

Are you a Christian? Are you assured of your salvation? If not, or if you'd like to know how to communicate the gospel to others, then I urge you to read the next chapter of this book.

I end this chapter with these words of magnificent praise, the lyrics of Charles Wesley:

> O for a thousand tongues to sing
> My great Redeemer's praise,
> The glories of my God and King,
> The triumphs of His grace.
>
> Jesus! the name that charms our fears,
> That bids our sorrows cease;
> 'Tis music in the sinner's ears,
> 'Tis life, and health, and peace.
>
> He breaks the power of canceled sin,
> He sets the prisoner free;
> His blood can make the foulest clean;
> His blood availed for me.

Reflections for the season

1. Are you satisfied with your patterns of giving?

2. Examine your attitude when giving. Are you joyful?

3. Would you say that you give sparingly or bountifully?

4. Have you received God's gift of His Son?

Christmas Morning

$\mathscr{I}$t's 5:30 on Christmas morning when I roll out of bed, letting Pearl snatch a few extra minutes of sleep for a change. The gray sky will soon surrender to the pinks and yellows of the dawn. It's a family tradition for me to prepare breakfast on Christmas Day, so in robe and slippers I trudge into the kitchen to begin mixing the batter for the whole wheat pecan waffles we'll have.

Soon freshly-ground coffee is perking; a pitcher of chilled orange juice made with spring water rests on the counter; pork sausages sizzle in the frying pan on the stove; waffles are crisping in the waffle iron. The aroma wafts through the house, stirring the six sleepyheads to activity. The back door opens and in walk our oldest daughter and her husband who live nearby. Our two-and-a-half-year-old grandson bounds out of the bedroom to begin toying with the unwrapped train set under the tree. Our one-year-old grandbaby still sleeps.

"Time for breakfast!" I call from the kitchen. Then Pearl, who by this time has joined me, begins serving platters of waffles covered with blueberries and piled high with sausages. We eat in shifts, and stack the dirty dishes in the sink. There will be time for such mundane things as dishwashing later. Besides, the kids can't wait to get to the presents!

Our other daughter and her husband arrive, and it is finally time to gather 'round the twinkling tree. Grandson Ian fidgets in his Aunt Julea's lap, while his baby brother Andrew, now awake, scoots around in his walker, oblivious to the reasons behind the excitement. Grandpa (that's me) sits in his rocker with his Bible open to Luke chapter 2, and begins to speak, "We need to remember, in the midst of these packages, why we are here. Let me read you the story of the first Christmas." And so I open the Bible to the familiar account:

> About this time, Caesar Augustus, the Roman Emperor, decreed that a census should be taken throughout the nation. (This census was taken when Quirinius was governor of Syria.)
>
> Everyone was required to return to his ancestral home for this registration. And because Joseph was a member of the royal line, he had to go to Bethlehem in Judea, King David's ancient home—journeying there from the Galilean village of Nazareth. He took with him Mary, his fiancee, who was obviously pregnant by this time.
>
> And while they were there, the time came for her baby to be born; and she gave birth to her first child, a son. She wrapped him in a blanket and laid him in a manger, because there was no room for them in the village inn.
>
> That night some shepherds were in the fields outside the village, guarding their flocks of sheep. Suddenly an angel appeared among them, and the landscape shone bright with the glory of the Lord. They were badly frightened, but the angel reassured them.
>
> "Don't be afraid!" he said. "I bring you the most joyful news ever announced, and it is for everyone! The Savior—yes, the Messiah, the Lord—has been born

tonight in Bethlehem! How will you recognize him? You will find a baby wrapped in a blanket, lying in a manger!

Suddenly, the angel was joined by a vast host of others—the armies of heaven—praising God:

"Glory to God in the highest heaven," they sang, "and peace on earth for all those pleasing him" (Luke 2:1-14 TLB).

"Grandpa, can we open the presents now?" asks my energetic older grandson.

"Not just yet, Ian . . . there's more to come. Be patient!"

"Okay."

FROM BETHLEHEM TO CALVARY, GOD'S CHRISTMAS TREE

But before we finish our Christmas morning visit at the Andersons', there are a few thoughts I'd like to share with those of you reading this. It is my sincere hope that you fully comprehend the significance of that first Christmas morning. The humble birth in the simple stable was absolutely vital to our eternal well being.

God had no choice but to intervene in human history if He were going to retrieve the relationship with man, His creature, which had been lost in the garden of Eden. The mission of reconciliation begun in Bethlehem was accomplished at the cross of Calvary. God is now free to offer you the gift of salvation, because His requirements of justice and holiness have been fully satisfied by the death and resurrection of His Son.

Salvation is a package under God's Christmas tree which has been wrapped specially for you. Your name is on the tag. Let me tell you how to take the gift and make it your own. In so doing, I'd like to briefly focus on three concepts: the reason for Christmas, the remedy of Christmas, and the result of Christmas.

THE REASON FOR CHRISTMAS: SIN

The reason for Christmas is the sin of man. Man's sinful nature separates him from a relationship with a righteous and completely holy God. Try and try as we may, we cannot, under our own human power, become totally free of sin in our thoughts and actions. It is impossible.

According to the Bible, sin infects every man and woman (except the God-man, Jesus Christ). In the words of Romans 3:23, "For all have sinned and fall short of the glory of God" (NASB).

Not only does sin infiltrate our lives, but it carries with it an awesome penalty: death—eternal separation from a perfect, holy, just God. Writes Paul in Romans 5:12, "Therefore, just as through one man sin entered into the world, and death through sin, and so death spread to all men, because all sinned" (NASB).

And yet because God loves us, there is hope for escaping the penalty of our disobedience. This hope is found in Jesus Christ. Romans 6:23 puts it this way, "For the wages of sin is death, but the free gift of God is eternal life in Christ Jesus our Lord" (NASB).

THE REMEDY OF CHRISTMAS: THE SACRIFICE

The remedy for man's problem of sin is found in a sacrifice, specifically the sacrifice of Jesus Christ upon the cross of Calvary.

Under the Jewish legal and religious system, animals were slain, their blood shed, their carcasses offered upon the altar in acts of atonement for man's sin. Yet after the resurrection of Christ, such forms of sacrifice became invalid, because a far greater sacrifice had been put to death at Calvary. Hebrews 10:4 tells us, "For it is impossible for the blood of bulls and goats to take away sins" (NASB).

Instead, Jesus Christ carried the weight of our sins to the

cross. He was slain, His blood shed, so that He might pay the penalty of our disobedience, our rebellion, our selfishness, our sin. Christ functioned as the lamb of sacrifice on our behalf. As John the Baptist proclaimed when Jesus approached, "Behold, the Lamb of God, who takes away the sin of the world!" (John 1:29 NASB).

Isaiah 53:5, prophetically speaking of the Messiah, Jesus Christ, says, "But He was pierced through for our transgressions, He was crushed for our iniquities; The chastening for our well-being fell upon Him, And by His scourging we are healed" (NASB).

Romans 5:8 states, "But God demonstrates His own love toward us, in that while we were yet sinners, Christ died for us" (NASB).

Hebrews 10:10 says Christians have "been sanctified through the offering of the body of Jesus Christ once for all" (NASB; see also Hebrews 10:5,12).

And 1 Peter 1:18-19 reminds believers that they "were not redeemed with perishable things like silver or gold . . . but with precious blood, as of a lamb unblemished and spotless, the blood of Christ" (NASB; see also Isaiah 53:4, 2 Corinthians 5:14-15, Colossians 1:20).

THE RESULT OF CHRISTMAS: SALVATION

The ultimate result of Christmas is that salvation is made available through this sacrifice of Christ which was necessitated because of man's sin. Reconciliation with God is now possible! Salvation is offered as a gift, through faith in the Lord Jesus.

John 3:16 says, "For God so loved the world, that He gave His only begotten Son, that whoever believes in Him should not perish, but have eternal life" (NASB).

Ephesians 2:8-9 puts it this way: "For by grace you have been saved through faith; and that not of yourselves, it is a gift of God" (NASB).

God is waiting for our responses. He longs for us to turn to Him in faith and receive the gift of Christ. 2 Peter 3:9 states: "The Lord is not slow about His promise, as some count slowness, but is patient toward you, not wishing for any to perish but for all to come to repentance" (NASB).

The gift is ready. Anyone who comes may grasp it. It is a universal offer whereby we may be forgiven our sins and declared perfectly, perpetually righteous in God's sight. It is the only passport to heaven. It is the sole means by which we can experience fellowship with God now and forevermore.

Revelation 22:17 says, "And the Spirit and the bride say, 'Come.' And let the one who hears say, 'Come.' And let the one who is thirsty come; let the one who wishes take the water of life without cost" (NASB). Have you done that? Have you made that decision for Christ? It is an open invitation. Remember that Jesus Himself says in Revelation 3:20, "Behold, I stand at the door and knock; if anyone hears My voice and opens the door, I will come in to him, and will dine with him, and he with Me" (NASB).

He is ready and waiting. It is your move.

GRASPING THE GIFT

Will you come to Jesus Christ today? Perhaps you are saying, "How?" Speak to the Lord in prayer, and do three things as you pray to Him:

1 Acknowledge your sin to God. Admit that you have fallen short of His perfect standards, His righteous holiness.

2. Accept by faith the sacrifice of Christ for your sin.

3. Affirm the fact, by thanking him, that salvation is yours.

Prayer is just talking to God as you would to a friend. Tell Him that you are a sinner and that you believe that the Lord Jesus died for you. Tell Him that you are trusting Christ for the forgiveness of your sins. Then thank Him for coming into your life and making you His child. That's it! It's done.

It is good to record this decision for future assurance. Perhaps you might want to do so in your Bible, or even in the blanks below:

Name _____, I received Jesus Christ as Savior on Day _____,
Month _____, Year _____, Time _____.
Signed _____

WELCOME TO THE FAMILY!

Once you are "born again," salvation is yours eternally. You will never be "unborn." You will never lose the gift. As Jesus says in John 10:27-28, "My sheep hear My voice, and I know them, and they follow Me; and I give eternal life to them, and they shall never perish; and no one shall ever snatch them out of My hand" (NASB, see also John 10:29).

It's time to grab your Bible and learn more about the Lord who has just come into your life. May I suggest you begin by reading through the Gospel of John? And here also are some verses to look up which will get you going in the right direction:

1. 1 John 5:11-12
2. John 16:24
3. 1 Corinthians 10:13
4. 1 John 1:9
5. Proverbs 3:5-6

Next, find yourself a solid, Bible-teaching, Bible-believing church in which to worship. If there is a conservative, evangelical organization such as Bible Study Fellowship in your area, join up, too! Spending time with other Christians is essential to every believer!

Finally, I'd like to leave you with the thoughts of the apostle Paul, who closes his letter to the Philippians with these words:

> And my God shall supply all your needs according to His riches in glory in Christ Jesus.
>
> Now to our God and Father be the glory forever and ever. Amen. . .
>
> . . . The grace of the Lord Jesus Christ be with your spirit (Philippians 4:19-20,23).

And may this be the happiest, most blessed, most meaningful Christmas yet for you!

MEANWHILE, BACK AT THE ANDERSONS'

The Christmas story from Luke 2 completed, I pick up a beautifully-illustrated volume which has become a treasure to our family. It contains a poem written by our good friend and member of our Ministries' board, Bill Dunn.

It has become a part of our Christmas tradition to read aloud *The Christmas Tree* before tearing into the packages under our own shining evergreen. Bill's work serves as one more reminder that Jesus is the reason for the season! With his kind permission, I have reprinted the poem for your enjoyment this, and perhaps every, Christmas Day.

Picture, if you will, a snow-swept dairy farm in North Texas. It is Christmas Eve, 1941, and a little boy named Billy is spending the holidays with his beloved grandparents, whom he calls Mama and Dad. Thus begins the story of an unforgettable day in the heart and mind of a small boy who

so eagerly looks forward to finding the perfect Christmas
tree, and who encounters along the way the rich wisdom of a
godly grandfather.

"Wake up! Wake up, you little sleepy head.
It's time to cut that Christmas tree," old Dad said.

Under a quilted mountain I greeted the dawn.
With sleep filled eyes and a great big yawn.

"It's that time already?" I mumbled slow.

"Yep, and looks like we got to cut it in the snow."

"Snow!" I yelled, kicking quilts left and right.

"Yep," said Dad, "Looks like it snowed all night."

I hopped and skipped across the cold wood floor,
Out my room and opened the porch door.
Like soft cotton velvet spread everywhere,
Brightly sun-kissed and shadowed here and there,
There lay the yard, the fields, and barns,
The trees lightly strung with white yarns,
The fences, the creekline, the fluffy hills,
And the haystacks sitting like big white pills.

"Now shut the door and come on in, Son,
We'll go out when breakfast is done."

Biscuit and bacon flavors filled the air,
While I got dressed and combed my hair.
Then I joined Dad and Mama, Mac and Jack,
For a meal that made others look like a snack.

They had already milked eighty head of cows,
Fed the chickens, got the eggs, and slopped the sows.

A giant plate of bacon and two bowls of eggs,
Two big pans of biscuits and syrup in kegs,
A platter of butter and two pitchers of milk,
With that snow outside like satin and silk,
The aroma of hot coffee, talk of chores and work,
Mama fussing and busy like a Saturday night clerk.
Right after eating, Mac and Jack went to town
To deliver the raw milk on the regular round.

"Now get your coat, Son, let's be on our way.
We'll find the finest tree out there today."

Mama stopped all her kitchen work and said,

"Now before you go out you make up your bed,
And wear your galoshes and put a hat on your head.
I got too much to do without you turning up dead!"

Mama bundled me up so heavy and snug,
Then gave me a kiss and a great big hug.

Dad and I started out walking real fast.
He didn't say where to and I didn't ask.
Past the smokehouse and the dairy barn,
The chicken houses, hog pen, and hay barn,
We made our way toward the pasture land,
Stomping single file as if to a band.
I carried the hatchet and Dad the axe,
As we moved west with the sun to our backs.

"Dad, You gonna let me cut it down?"

"Do I let you go with me to town?
You betcha! We'll find one just right for you.
I'm counting on you to chop it clean through!"

"Oh Dad, I'll do it real good, you can bet.
You ain't ever seen a chopper like me yet!"

"Well, them old evergreens are awful tough,
But I won't help unless it really gets rough."

We came to the creek with iced-over pools,
Just trickles of water in the middle and slews.
We stepped across on a rotting old log
And a couple of rocks near the springtime bog.
Nudging the crystal grass that lay by the bank,
We trudged our way past an old stock tank.

Where Dad was going then I could see,
A line of evergreens right in front of me.

This was a part of the farm I'd never seen,
This slope with the line of evergreen.
I caught up with Dad and got ahead.

"Be careful with that hatchet!" Old Dad said.

As fast as I could, I went from tree to tree,
Saying at each one, "This one looks great to me!"
In and out that line of trees, I ran and ran,
Laughing and yelling, "This is great! This is grand!"

Then I saw it near the top of the hill,
Standing tall and straight, perfectly still.
Like a picture of a Christmas card scene,
Or a painting from the cover of a POST magazine,

On a stout trunk sat that triangle of green,
The most beautiful Christmas tree I'd ever seen.
It commanded respect from its place on the slope
And made me think of beauty, power and hope.

When Dad caught up, I was just standing there.
All I could do was just look and stare.
It towered before me like a majestic king.

"My, my, ain't that one there a pretty thing.
I think it'll just fit." I heard Dad say.
"Best get started if we're to finish today."

Up to that tree and around the other side,
Old Dad trudged with the axe by his side.
After sizing it up for a little bit,
He began to chop and I hurt when he hit.
A few of the lower limbs he cut away,
Notched the trunk, then turned to me to say,
"There's the bare trunk. Are you ready to start?"
I stepped forward with sorrow in my heart.

Tears welled up in my eyes to see that tree,
Knowing that it was hurting because of me.
At Dad's urging I started in on one side,
But everytime I hit it, I thought I'd die.

Then I threw down the hatchet, yelling, "I can't!
Oh Dad, I can't! I just can't! I just can't!
Who am I to kill it? Oh, who am I?
How could anybody want this tree to die?
It's too lovely and great to be chopped down.
Can't we go and buy one back in town?"

Old Dad stood there, looking down at me.
With tear-blurred eyes, I could barely see,

When he stepped over and held me tight.
Although it was daytime, for me it was night.
The harder I tried to stop, the more I cried,
While Dad hugged me closer to his side.
How long we stood there, I still don't know,
A grandpa and a crying little boy in the snow.

"It's too late, Son, I really hate to say.
We've already cut it too much of the way.
I would've bought you every tree in town,
If only I'd known this would get you down.
Wouldn't it be better than leavin' it to die
To carry it to the house with you and I?
I'll build it a good base so it can stand tall.
We'll put it by the front living room wall."

"Will it really die out here, no matter what?"

"Yes, Son, it will and it'll suffer a lot."

"If we take it home, won't it die there too?"

"But not alone. It'll be there with me and you."

"Oh, Dad, I don't want to see it again.
The thing I've done is a real bad sin."

"I'm glad that you've got a tender heart,
But now you've got to be a man and do your part."

"Okay, Dad, if that's what I got to do,
But the rest of the chopping is up to you."

Dad took his axe while I turned my back
And I heard the cruel echoes of crack, crack, crack!

Then I watched as the tree fell to the snow,
And heard Dad saying, "Now get the top, Son, let's go."

As we walked away I looked back at the slope.
Gone was the tree of beauty, power, and hope.

On the way back, Dad didn't say much,
And I choked everytime I felt the tree's touch.
Its branches would bounce as we carried it along,
Brushing my face and I'd feel anew the wrong.
We stopped by the barn, bleak as a bone,
And Dad made a cross for the tree to sit on;
Then on to the house and the living room,
Standing up the tree for its final doom.

There it stood, its regal nobility gone,
Dead and dying, sacrificed for a song,
A tune for Christmas, for fun, gifts and cheer,
But it had lost its life which had to be dear.

"It looks very nice there, don't it, Son?"

"No, Dad, it's a real bad thing I've done.
It had to be happier up there on the hill
Than sitting in this house, dying and still."

I ran to my room and fell on my bed,
Grieving for the tree that now was dead.
Dad followed and sat down by my side.
While Mama took a chair, breathed and sighed.

"Now, Son, I reckon I know how you feel,
But can I tell you about some things
    that are real?"

Now, I knew Dad had wisdom, was kind and good.
I'd always listen to him like I knew I should.

"I know you know a lot about Jesus Christ,
How He's God's Son, our Saviour, the Christ.
What we did to this tree was done to Him,
And He didn't fight them that were hurting Him.
Just like this tree gave in to our axe,
He gave Himself up to the pain that wracks.
He suffered that death for you and Mama and me
To save us and open our eyes to see.
Upon a throne like that tree on the slope,
He willingly came down to become our hope.
At Christmas time we celebrate His birth,
But He really came to die for us here on earth;
For all—rich, poor, man, woman, girl, and boy—
To give each of us a life filled with joy.
This tree did that and you'll see on the morn.
When we celebrate the day that Christ was born."

Dad left the room and I curled up real tight,
And Mama said, "Tomorrow, you'll see Dad is right."

Mac and Jack came by and Mama and Dad too,
But I cried and hurt the whole night through.
I wouldn't help them decorate the tree,
Just the pain and death was all I could see;
No supper, no dessert, no cookies or treats;
Only the tear-soaked pillow that grief often meets.

It was about dawn, I think, when I awoke,
Lifting my head from a pillow that was soaked.
There was a dim gray light coming in from outside
And nothing moving and all quiet inside.

I got up and tip-toed to the living room.
What I saw was not pain and death or doom!

Decorated with balls, lights, all sorts of things,
That tree just glowed with an aura that sings!
All around the base were packages and gifts,
The pain and hurt lost in the spirit that lifts.
Dad and Mama came in, so did Mac and Jack,
And we all stood there gazing, taken aback.

"Dad, I think I see what you mean.
We took it from that line of evergreen
And, although it had to give up its life,
It now brings great joy into our life."

"Just like Jesus Christ, my dear Son,
He came to do a job and got it done."

I looked back at that tree, sensed its joy,
And knew He'd died for me too, only a boy.

That was a Christmas a long time ago,
But it stuck in my head in a way you'll know.
It sunk its roots way down in me deep
And gave me this treasure that I can't but keep—
I was never again to look at a tree
Without thinking of Christ Who died for me.

(M. B. Bill Dunn)

Chambers, Oswald. 1935. *My Utmost for His Highest.* New York: Dodd, Mead, and Company, Inc.

Dunn, M. B. 1985. *A Body of Work: Part II, The Christmas Tree.* Euless, Texas: BDC Service Corporation.

Elliott, Emily E. S. "Thou Didst Leave Thy Throne."

Francis of Assisi. "All Creatures of Our God and King." Translated by William H. Draper. J. Curwin and Sons, Ltd.

Hengstenberg, E. W. 1970. *Christology of the Old Testament and a Commentary on the Messianic Predictions.* Grand Rapids, Michigan: Kregel Publications.

Howe, Julia Ward. "Battle Hymn of the Republic."

Ironside, H. A. 1952. *Expository Notes on the Prophet Isaiah.* Neptune, New Jersey: Loizeaux Brothers, Inc.

Keller, W. Phillip. 1977. *Rabboni.* Old Tappan, New Jersey: Fleming H. Revell Company.

King, Guy H. 1952. *Joy Way: An Expositional Application of the Epistle to the Philippians.* Fort Washington, Pennsylvania: Christian Literature Crusade.

Lindsey, Hal. 1974. *The Promise.* Irvine, California: Harvest House Publishers.

McDowell, Josh. 1972. *Evidence That Demands a Verdict.* Arrowhead Springs, Colorado: Campus Crusade for Christ, Inc.

Motes, Edward. "The Solid Rock."

Newton, John. "Amazing Grace! How Sweet the Sound."

Oakeley, Frederick, trans. "O Come All Ye Faithful."

Stedman, Ray C. 1982. *Expository Studies in 2 Corinthians.* Waco, Texas: Word Books.

Tan, Paul Lee. 1979. *Encyclopedia of 7,700 Illustrations: Signs of the Times.* Rockville, Maryland: Assurance Publishers.

Tournier, Paul. 1963. *The Seasons of Life.* Translated by John S. Gilmour. Atlanta: John Knox Press.

Unger, Merrill F. 1966. *Unger's Bible Dictionary.* Chicago: Moody Press.

Walvoord, John F. 1969. *Jesus Christ Our Lord.* Chicago: Moody Press.

Walvoord, John F. and Roy B. Zuck, eds. 1983. *The Bible Knowledge Commentary, New Testament Edition.* Wheaton, Illinois: Victor Books.

————. 1985. *The Bible Knowledge Commentary, Old Testament Edition.* Wheaton, Illinois: Victor Books.

Wesley, Charles. "O for a Thousand Tongues to Sing."

Wilkinson, Kate. "May the Mind of Christ, My Saviour."

DON ANDERSON MINISTRIES

Popular pastor, teacher, and conference speaker, Don Anderson tours Texas and neighboring states giving Bible classes and business luncheon seminars during the fall, winter, and spring months. During the summer, Don Anderson Ministries staffs many youth and family camps. Don also preaches regularly at two churches staffed by the Ministries and speaks at conferences in various locations in the United States and Canada. His audiences of business and professional men and women, housewives and tradespeople, testify that his refreshing teaching makes the Scriptures "come alive" for them.

Don Anderson graduated from Northwestern College in 1955 with a bachelor of arts degree and received his master's degree from Dallas Theological Seminary. He has been in Christian ministry for over thirty years, serving as a Young Life staff member, youth pastor, program director at the Firs Bible and Missionary Conference, executive director of Pine Cove Conference Center and, since 1972, has served as director of the nonprofit organization, Don Anderson Ministries, headquartered in Tyler, Texas.

Don Anderson has many audio and video cassette tapes, based on his teachings, which are produced by the Ministries and distributed widely. There is also a Ministries newsletter, *The Grapevine,* which reaches about eight thousand homes.

If you'd like to enhance your study of the Scriptures, the cassette tape series on *A Gift Too Wonderful for Words* is available from the author. If you are interested in hearing Don's teachings, please write to this address for a free tape catalog.

> Don Anderson Ministries
> Station A, Box 6611
> Tyler, Texas 75711